LIVING FLORAL

LIVING FLORAL

Entertaining and Decorating with Flowers

MARGOT SHAW

WITH KAREN M. CARROLL AND LYDIA SOMERVILLE
DESIGN BY ELLEN SHANKS PADGETT

FOREWORD BY CHARLOTTE MOSS

RIZZOLI
NEW YORK

New York · Paris · London · Milan

DEDICATION

This book is dedicated to my beloved husband—farmer, pastor, mentor, counselor, friend—and to the One who brought us together.

CONTENTS

FOREWORD: FLORAL MEMORIES

Charlotte Moss

I asked Margot Shaw for some advice years ago, long before I knew that she was one of the most straight-shooting, down-to-earth Southern women around. She was born and bred in Birmingham with a little time in Connecticut, Switzerland, and college via Virginia—my neck of the woods—and we have been bonded by that honesty ever since.

I was asked to give a talk at the antiques show held at Birmingham's beautiful botanical gardens. The auditorium was filled with antiques buyers, dealers, decorating enthusiasts, and Margot, one of the sponsors of the event. On the plane or once home I asked myself the question, "What could I have done better or differently?" Anyone who has ever questioned or analyzed how he or she did something knows that self-analysis can be a tortuous, lonely exercise, so I picked up the phone and called Margot and put the question to her. Margot was clear, measured, thoughtful, and incredibly helpful with her brief response. Her answer: "Make it personal—people can always read the book. They came to hear you and about you." Now, whenever I am preparing a talk, that advice—that little voice in my head—guides me.

Since that time, we have traveled together and toured houses and gardens in England. We have spoken at the same events, done panels from Atlanta to Houston, and talked into the night after dinner. We have had dinner in East Hampton and laughed all night together with our husbands. Now, as a contributor to *Flower,* her magazine, I have the opportunity to propose story ideas to Margot, my boss. She is still dispensing advice, I am still listening, and we both are still laughing. We are further bonded by our love of all things floral, gardens and the people who create them, and just the enjoyment of being amid flowers. *Living Floral: Entertaining and Decorating with Flowers* is the perfect way for Margot to share more of her world with us.

Scroll back a few years when I called Margot and said, "Let's put a group together to see Nancy Lancaster's three houses in England." Phone calls back and forth, invitations extended, our travel advisor Indagare engaged, date set, and off we went to stay at Ditchley and have private tours of the other houses and gardens, those places that Nancy created on English soil with her indomitable American spirit and highly evolved instinct for all things beautiful. Nancy would herself claim that she was "always searching for beauty." Her three room essentials have become the mantra of her disciples: "a fire, candlelight, and flowers." It is, of course, that last item that brought us together.

Margot had an idea and the determination to create a magazine to honor flowers: how they are grown, glorified, coveted, painted, and memorialized. Flowers beautify and unify just as Margot has spent her adult life, spreading her gospel of beauty and making converts along the way. Beauty, of course, is indefinable—beauty is in the eyes of the beholder, or so we have learned. The joy one receives by encountering things that embody their definition of beauty is exhilarating; it's a joy that lovers of all things beautiful want to share. Margot is one of those people who shares, and she boldly decided to create *Flower,* her magazine that delivers that message.

Now she has compiled some of her favorites between these two covers, the pages of which will no doubt soon be filled with Post-it Notes. Like Nancy Lancaster, Margot has been "always searching for beauty," and for her, it is, in a word, the flower.

INTRODUCTION

Margot Shaw

"Everybody needs beauty as well as bread, places to play in and pray in, where Nature may heal and cheer and give strength to body and soul alike," said John Muir, the nineteenth- and early twentieth-century American naturalist, author, and early environmentalist.

I recall traveling as a newlywed (second time around) to the mountains of North Carolina with my husband, who had booked us into "a wonderful Victorian bed and breakfast" to hear him tell it. So, after a six-hour drive from Alabama, we arrived. The exterior was charming and the gardens lovely, which boded well. My new husband delivered me to our room and then left to park the car. I stood looking around the room that was decorated from head to toe in mauve with cream-colored synthetic doilies on every piece of furniture with arms, a back, or a flat surface; a stellar series of velvet cat paintings; and a dresser and bookcases filled with tacky tchotchkes.

When my husband returned to the room, I was locked in the bathroom, crying softly, distressed at the prospect of spending five days there, but not wanting him to think I was a spoiled brat. He finally coaxed me out of the loo and into confessing the source of my distress. At the end of my litany of complaints, he got on the phone and called a storied mountain resort down the road a bit, where he had vacationed as a child, and booked us in for the duration of the trip.

Our room was plain and simple, with white chenille spreads on twin beds, floral chintz bistro curtains, and a chest of drawers no doubt procured from a yard sale. The floor was slanted but painted a cool and summery forest green. There was an exposed lightbulb hanging from the center of the room's ceiling

HOW I LIVE WITH FLOWERS

Garden gathering: My husband is the gardener and I cut what he grows. There's always something to clip and arrange—whether French blue hydrangeas in the summer, white nandina berries and remontant roses in the fall, camellias in the winter, Lenten roses in late winter, and forsythia and tulips in the spring, among other blooms and branches.

Random acts of arranging: I let the flowers that I cut and bring in do the talking. I also take delight in repurposing unlikely vessels into vases, like a small tole waste basket filled with an arrangement of hydrangeas, a silver Revere bowl with floating gardenias, a glass art bottle with one lone branch of forsythia or quince. As a Southerner, I'm partial to magnolia leaves. Our property is bordered on one side with magnolias. I cut and arrange the branches in the grate of my fireplace in summer. They're glossy and lush, and prettier than the fire screen.

Party flowers: Depending on how much time I have, I will cut from the garden, and place flowers all around the house before a party. If it's a special event, I'll call in the professionals.

Wall flowers: The powder room is such an ideal spot for a punch of color and pattern. In ours, I used a bold tomato, charcoal, and cream chinoiserie paper that features vines and flowers throughout—such a perfect nod to nature without being too overt.

but also a jaunty little gourd lamp on the bedside table. Not the Ritz, by any means; however, it had history, character, and no pretense. But best of all, there was no mauve, no lace, and no velvet paintings. My body and soul were indeed content in this place of rustic beauty.

This episode should not have come as a surprise to me. Since I was a child, I have responded to beauty. I was raised by very stylish and cultured parents who wanted me to experience and embrace beauty everywhere. I remember as a child of five being taken to the Louvre to view Leonardo da Vinci's masterpiece, the *Mona Lisa,* and being pretty underwhelmed by the somewhat homely woman set in a drab-colored background in what seemed a very small painting. My father registered my disappointment and instinctively grabbed my hand and led me through great halls, down stairs, around corners, and finally to the crescendo of the Winged Victory of Samothrace at the top of a mountain of steps. There she stood, this headless, timeless goddess of victory, bathed in a shaft of natural light. Stunning, literally. Almost sixty years later, I can remember feeling exhilarated and a calm at the same time. This sensation was repeated countless times throughout my young life as I experienced the joy of learning a Debussy piece for the piano in grade school; of sitting in the audience of the Winter Garden Theatre on Broadway as Angela Lansbury embodied Mame; the pleasure of my blue toile bedroom; and even the iconic smell of the dark liver chestnut coat of my pony Gypsy,

who though quite corpulent, could fly over four-foot jumps—and somehow we looked and I felt graceful doing it.

I have always responded to beauty in nature as well. I recall rambling through the woods on the Alabama mountain where I grew up, happening upon a carpet of different-colored hyacinths in a neighbor's garden and admiring them so much that I proceeded to pick every last one and take them home. The delight of those beautiful and fragrant flowers was worth the punishment—a hairbrush to the backside—meted out by my less-than-enthusiastic mother when I arrived home.

The urge to gather flowers and all forms of beauty into our lives is, I think, primordial, and in my view, began in a garden. So, how fitting that we should be inspired by living surrounded by natural beauty. Whether fresh from the garden or hundreds of years old on a *papier peint,* flowers lend a richness and romance to living and celebrating life that is undeniable. It must be said that, in my experience, especially in the darker seasons of my life, beauty, and especially natural beauty, has buoyed me in an almost supernatural way. Georgia O'Keeffe once said, "If I could paint that flower in a huge scale, then you could not ignore its beauty." And as editor in chief of *Flower* magazine, I pretty much spend my days and many nights trying to ensure that readers cannot ignore the natural beauty of flowers and gardens, outside and in.

In this book, we paint and elevate flowers with words and pictures, looking at creative and talented

OPPOSITE, CLOCKWISE FROM TOP LEFT: Flowers and herbs bunched in burlap-covered vases keep things casual. I arrange flowers for the centerpiece in the spot where it will be placed. I always include something heirloom on my table, in this case, my mother's bamboo flatware in an herb pot. Napkins by Les Indiennes round out the informal vibe. PREVIOUS PAGE: A lush and loose arrangement by friend Sybil Sylvester in my foyer.

people from the worlds of interior, garden, floral, and event design, as well as architecture and gastronomy, through a botanical lens. We are invited into their homes, gardens, and parties, to soak in and glean from their own personal floral aesthetics. Whether they are proponents of high style, simple rusticity, or a combination of the two, all of these tastemakers incorporate flowers in ways that appear effortless, gracious, and most of all, beautiful. It is my fondest hope that all who linger on these pages will find inspiration and experience the salutary gift of natural beauty.

My bedroom is washed in an early Shabby Chic floral fabric. It's like waking in a blue rose bower. Flowers by Sybil Sylvester.

SUMMER

SEA ISLAND PUNCH

Elaine Griffin
Brunswick, Georgia

Interior designer Elaine Griffin creates spaces that display a deft and often bold use of color and a global design perspective garnered during her ten years working as a fashion publicist, representing Ferragamo, Krizia, Céline, and Givenchy, and living in Paris and New York City. Her rooms are sophisticated, inviting, and tailored with a fashion maven's sense of attention to detail. "As a Southerner in New York City, I had long advised my friends on matters of decor and etiquette, so I enrolled in the New York School of Interior Design," says Elaine. After graduating, she worked for Peter Marino's senior architect. Griffin's company is now based in her hometown of Brunswick, Georgia, where her father was a groundbreaking African American general practitioner in medicine.

The many facets of Elaine's effervescent personality become evident when she entertains. For a luncheon for friends at the Sea Island resort, she summoned the ultimate preppy icon Lilly Pulitzer as her inspiration. "As a lifelong Southern preppy, Lilly's shift dresses are my summer wardrobe staple," she says, "so I chose one of her fabric designs for the tablecloth and opted to wear white instead of my usual patterned shift, because who wants to clash with her table linens?"

Elaine usually favors multiple small floral arrangements rather than a single centerpiece. But the Georgian Room courtyard demanded a stronger statement, so Elaine worked with Kelly Revels and Bryce Vann Brock of The Vine to create a tabletop garden worthy of the setting. Lavish, lush, and bursting with color, the arrangement is as ebullient as

the hostess's personality. Elaine added more personal touches with china, flatware, and linen napkins from home. "Starched linens are just one way Southerners say, 'I love you,'" she says. "Entertaining is about sharing a bit of ourselves with people we care about."

ABOVE: Jessica Zigman, head bartender of the Georgian Room, created two floral-inspired cocktails for Elaine Griffin's luncheon: Lavender Clouds and R&Rs (raspberry and rosewater). RIGHT: Elaine decorated the bar table with citrus fruits, tropical leaves, gloriosa lilies, and gardenia topiaries. A classic Lilly Pulitzer fabric design used as a tablecloth establishes a Southern preppy vibe. PREVIOUS PAGE: Elaine prefers a rectangular table with no more than eight guests because it's more conducive to intimate conversation.

LEFT: Floral, landscape, and event designers Kelly Revels and Bryce Vann Brock fashioned the elaborate centerpiece using ranunculuses, peonies, and calla lilies, inspired by the Lilly Pulitzer Heritage Floral tablecloth. Bamboo flatware emphasizes the tropical flair of the tablecloth. Clusters of ranunculuses in bud vases bring hints of color at eye level to the table. FOLLOWING SPREAD, LEFT PAGE, CLOCKWISE FROM TOP LEFT: "Even adults love party favors," says Elaine. "They're a fun way to cap off an event." Cocktail napkins by Dot and Army celebrate Georgia's nickname, the Peach State. Elaine found the foo dogs at Home Goods and spray-painted them white. RIGHT PAGE: An arrangement brimming with ranunculuses, peonies, and stock adds to the exuberant table decoration.

23

ELAINE'S PICKS FOR LIVING FLORAL

ENTERTAINING

True Southerners are unanimous about one thing: manners.

The handwritten thank-you note on beautiful stationery is expected. And if there's a botanical motif scrolling through the monogram or border, so much the better.

I shamelessly whip out my best china, crystal, and flatware at the drop of a hat.

It's a myth that round tables are easiest for conversation, because once you go beyond forty-eight inches in diameter, you are shouting at those across from you.

GARDEN PARTY

Cornelia Guest
Old Westbury, New York

G racious living can be learned but in Cornelia Guest's case, it's part of her DNA. With design and gardening maven C. Z. Guest for a mother and the Duke and Duchess of Windsor as godparents, one might imagine a head start in the style department.

Some of Cornelia's childhood memories include doing her homework after school in Halston's New York apartment and playing games with Andy Warhol when he would visit Long Island. But her childhood also featured horseback riding and romping with family pets, both of which engendered in her a fierce love of animals. As an avid vegan, she has turned her passion into commercial ventures including "cruelty-free" fashion and vegan catering.

Though Cornelia moves comfortably through the worlds of high fashion and high society, she is also a self-confessed homebody, hosting small dinner parties where she cooks organic and vegan meals served on heirloom china and silver; and garden gatherings where she culls from her mother's collection of D. Porthault floral-printed tablecloths and cuts flowers from the garden for table arrangements.

Cornelia is devoted to living a flower-filled life. Lilly Pulitzer sundresses with vibrant floral patterns, bloom-covered linens, and fresh arrangements are mainstays of her summer style. She gathers peonies, dahlias, and roses from the garden and artfully places individual stems in antique apothecary bottles on a windowsill or marching down a dining room table. When asked about the orchids in the green plastic pots in the windows at Templeton, her family home, she quips, "My mother always left the orchids in their original pots—I figured, if it was good enough for her, it's good enough for me." She is very down-to-earth about her gardening skills. "When my mother died, I knew nothing about flowers and gardening. I turned to her experts and asked them to teach me. It's been a labor of love, and I think of her whenever I'm in the garden—and other times, too."

CORNELIA'S PICKS FOR LIVING FLORAL
ENTERTAINING

Don't redecorate a room or put your pets elsewhere—your guests are coming to your house, and it's where you live. Sharing a glimpse into your life is part of entertaining and is as important as all the other aspects of your party.

Since I am a committed vegan, my guests know that I'll be serving vegan meals. It's important to me that I serve delicious food, and whether you're vegan, vegetarian, or even a carnivore, be sure the food tastes and looks good.

Linens are like clothes—they're an opportunity to express one's taste and personality. I've been able to cull from my mother's extensive collection of linens through the years, from specially printed Porthault tablecloths for a playful outdoor feel to more formal Frette and Yves Delorme pieces. I'll even throw an Indian-print spread over a table if I'm having a casual party.

ABOVE: Cornelia Guest sets a summer outdoor luncheon with a vintage Porthault tablecloth, family silver, and informal stemware, all crowned with luscious garden roses, casually arranged in a Majolica-type lettuce-ware pitcher. OPPOSITE, CLOCKWISE FROM TOP LEFT: Heirloom Dodie Thayer lettuce ware pairs well with Cornelia's more formal floral china and keeps things casual. Cornelia peruses her collection of Porthault tablecloths, which both her mother, C. Z., and she have collected through the years. A fulsome bed of roses just beyond a bay window at Cornelia's ancestral home, Templeton. PREVIOUS SPREAD: For an alfresco feast in the oak allée, Cornelia threw a matelassé spread and cloth from Les Indiennes over the middle of the table just to soften the effect.

BEHIND THE HEDGE

Richard Keith Langham
Water Mill, New York

In an era when almost everything, including design, is widely accessible via the Internet and social media, and trends come and go before some even have time to acknowledge them, interior designer Richard Keith Langham is a refreshingly established name with a rich and timeless style. There is an erudite gravitas to his work, balanced by the adamant refusal to take himself too seriously. His roots are in the Deep South—Brewton, Alabama, to be exact, which he credits in part to his interest in interiors. "I used to say that when you grow up in a small town, there isn't anywhere to go but your own house, so it better be pretty. But there were actually a number of beautifully appointed houses that piqued my early interest," he says. Keith's resume includes Parsons School of Design, an early and invaluable apprenticeship with the design legend Mark Hampton, a significant stint with the English country house aficionado Keith Irvine, and a year spent studying in England.

So it's no surprise that his interiors speak with a decidedly British accent. When asked about his country house on Long Island, he breezily responds, "Oh, the 'Witch's Hat' house? It's nothing fancy, just a place for me to spend weekends and have casual suppers with friends . . . My house is a mishmash of castoffs from jobs, some heirlooms that need slipcovering, and the very first pair of Christopher Spitzmiller lamps." The design is like the essence of that nonchalant, faded elegance so unique to British sensibility. Tucked behind a signature Hamptons hedge, the chocolate-shingled, salmon-shuttered American Queen Ann–style "Witch's Hat" trumpets a sense of playfulness, charming all who approach.

LEFT: The painted white porch of Richard Keith Langham's "Witch's Hat" home nods to his growing up in the South, where light colors are used to cool things off in the summer. OPPOSITE: Antique wicker furniture was painted chocolate brown to match the exterior of the summer house, and the cushions are covered in a lively salmon stripe. PREVIOUS PAGE: Keith sets a cool and inviting table for one of his summer suppers, with an informal cluster of clematis spilling over the top of a pitcher.

On a spring or summer evening, the designer favors dining alfresco. The soirée generally begins with cool drinks and light hors d'oeuvres in his tented pavilion overlooking a pool framed by four plastic pink flamingos—a decidedly not-too-serious touch. Then guests amble over to the wraparound front porch and gather at a gracious round table for one of Langham's delicious and simple suppers of fresh cream of squash soup with scallions, chicken paillard, arugula and tomato salad, and asparagus—and for dessert, mango sorbet and gingersnap cookies.

There are always flowers on the table and throughout the house. The host either cuts from copious drifts of hydrangeas in the garden and loosely arranges the blooms in an assortment of witty and artistic containers, or calls in Bridge-hampton florist Michael Grim to work his magic for a more elaborate look. The table is always dressed in one of the designer's many exotic textiles found in his travels or a cheerful floral-print fabric repurposed as a tablecloth.

Keith's alfresco evenings are a rich stew of ocean breezes, candlelight, and a playlist of standards, jazz, and Motown, as well as good food, pretty flowers, and a steady stream of lively conversation. "I love an ambience that wraps its arms around you, where everyone feels welcome, and special, and just a little bit spoiled," says Keith. It's Southern hospitality on Long Island to a T.

ABOVE: The pool house, situated at the end of the lawn facing the pool, is dressed in blues and whites and provides a cool respite on a summer's day. LEFT: Pre-dinner drinks are often served in the tented pavilion by the pool. The plastic pink flamingos keep things playful and fun. FOLLOWING SPREAD, LEFT PAGE, CLOCKWISE FROM TOP LEFT: Keith loves the Southern accent of a magnolia bloom floating in a bowl paired with seashells and starfish from New England. Keith awaits his guests on the front porch. Peaches, a piece of coral, ceramic oyster shells, and plates await the staging of dinner on the porch. RIGHT PAGE: Michael Grim, of Bridgehampton Florists, created an informal arrangement of viburnums and mock orange for the pool house.

KEITH'S PICKS FOR LIVING FLORAL
ENTERTAINING

Entertaining out East during the summer months calls for really refreshing but simple drinks. I'll have a swath of juices and sparkling waters for those who don't partake in stronger drink, and a full bar and good wine selection for those who do. Occasionally, I'll come up with a fizzy, festive specialty cocktail that can also be served as a "mocktail."

People are the secret sauce. I like to have a guest list that's mixed and interesting. I also like to laugh and have fun, so I include friends who are clever and witty and a few who are beautiful. I do not include unpleasant people. I don't think anyone goes to a dinner party hoping to find themselves in the middle of a heated argument—and for those who do, they can host their own soirée. I do enjoy a lively discussion, but it cannot degenerate into verbal fisticuffs—that's just not good manners. Lighthearted nonsense is my favorite topic.

TROPICAL FLAIR

Renny Reynolds and Jack Staub
Manalapan, Florida

When you're born to create, you're not bound by the medium. As a matter of fact, Renny Reynolds and his partner, Jack Staub, are perfect illustrations of this truth. Renny, a lover of all things botanical from eight years old, later incorporated this passion into event design when it was still called party planning. Not just any parties, but the iconic ones at Studio 54 as well as extravaganzas like the Yves Saint Laurent Opium launch complete with Chinese junks with gold lamé sails. He then segued into floral design and opened the still sought-after and chic Park Avenue floral studio and shop Renny & Reed. Eventually bequeathing the business to his nephew, Reed McIvaine, Renny set out for greener pastures involving more garden design and horticulture.

Jack, an actor and playwright, found a lifelong passion in gardening and writing about gardens when he and Renny purchased an eighteenth-century Bucks County, Pennsylvania, farmhouse along with the hundred acres surrounding it. They lovingly restored the stone house and tamed the acreage into a veritable botanical wonderland. They open this masterpiece, Hortulus Farm, to the public in the spring and summer months. Jack, tired of grocery-store iceberg lettuce, began to dream of a vegetable garden. He then planted one and was hooked. His first garden book was dedicated to that experience and he's written many other garden books since.

Every fall, after pouring themselves into Hortulus for months, these two head south to their magical South Florida garden and flower-filled retreat. Christened Curlew Point, the pale lemon–colored Bermuda-style house is surrounded on three sides by the Intracoastal Waterway. And thanks to Mother Nature and the gardening wizardry of the duo, it's wrapped in

such lush and varied botanical fare that a trip to the flower wholesaler is an anomaly. A good thing, since these two have a love of entertaining, and they do it well and often. "We love to share the views, the gardens, the sunsets, the cloud formations, and even the occasional strolling iguana," says Renny. He creates fun and flamboyant tablescapes incorporating whimsical pieces like colored glass bottles containing stems of blooms or greenery found on the property, seashells, and crystal balls, with bright, festive table linens. While Renny sets the scene, Jack prepares one of his favorite warm weather dinners—always something uncomplicated but delicious, so that he's not cooped up in the kitchen during the party.

The inside of Curlew Point, filled with tropical flowers and plants, echoes the outside. In the foyer, beyond the tangerine lacquered front doors, sits a pedestal table that always boasts a frothy, welcoming arrangement of Curlew's finest flowers or fronds. And in the living room, the tray ceiling is hand-painted with whimsical elephant's-ear leaves woven into cane lattice-work, while a fresh bromeliad recaps the orange of the entrance and the double gourd lamps. "We have particularly enjoyed creating a tropical dream for our own enjoyment and the enjoyment of our guests," says Renny. "And of course, for our beloved rescue dogs, Bandit, Parker, and Sadie."

RIGHT: The entrance to Curlew Point provides an inviting preview of coming attractions: On the left, a giant terra-cotta pot brims with variegated sansevieria. Beyond it are a potted calamondin orange and an arbor draped in 'Orange Ice' bougainvillea, with pots of white elephant's-ear plants and a white phalaenopsis orchid. On the right, among other tropical plants, are elephant's-ear plants with black stems and an arborvitae hedge. PREVIOUS PAGE: Renny cuts from the garden for the table and weaves whimsical sea-themed accents and jewel-toned bottle vases into the mix.

RENNY AND JACK'S PICKS FOR LIVING FLORAL
ARRANGING AND ENTERTAINING

Hydrangeas are hardy and reliable flowers to grow for cutting. Cut them in early morning if possible, give the stems a little snip right before placing them in water so they'll drink more, and remove extra leaves so the blooms hydrate—they're not called hydrangeas for nothing.

Quick and easy flower arrangements add a little shimmer to the party. Fill the house with groups of small pots of flowering plants—large arrangements everywhere can tend to look funereal or, at the least, too distracting. The party is really about people.

The secret to a divine dinner party is lighting—it's key to a warm, comfortable ambience. Make sure the chandelier is dimmed, and candles are glowing all around.

Invite fun people who have something in common. Even if they've not met before, they'll enjoy being together.

Be relaxed—nothing kills the joy faster than a nervous host or hostess who's trying too hard. And if the soufflé falls or the power goes out, just laugh and your guests will too—order pizza, light more candles, and do an impromptu reading from a favorite book.

ABOVE: With the Intracoastal Waterway in the background, Bandit, one of Renny and Jack's rescue pups, relaxes on a bench by a fire pit in the late afternoon cool. Surrounding this seating area are, from right to left, a spicy jatropha with bright red blooms, a Ganges primrose, a giant Norfolk Island pine, and a coconut palm in the center. OPPOSITE, CLOCKWISE FROM TOP LEFT: Continuing the orange theme that starts at the front door and travels throughout the house, Renny and Jack decorated the guest room in warm tones of apricot with tobacco-colored accents. Botanical prints and a simple white phalaenopsis orchid on the cassone contribute a subtle floral presence. Seated from left to right, Bandit, Jack, Parker, Renny, and Sadie—the dogs are all rescues. A collar of 'Malbec' bromeliads under a graceful Norfolk Island pine picks up the pinks in the hammock stripe.

The living room, crowned by a hand-painted ceiling scene by artist Claudia Funke, is a festive mix of a matched set of "pretzel" rattan furniture by Paul T. Frankl; a mid-century ovoid molded-plastic tube lamp by R. Rougier; treasures from friends and travels, including nineteenth-century cast-iron Buddhas; and a mirror decorated with scads of shells, one of Jack's many creative contributions.

CULTIVATING BEAUTY

Elizabeth Locke
Boyce, Virginia

Jewelry designer Elizabeth Locke knows how to design a beautiful setting. She scours the globe for vibrant cabochon stones, luminous Venetian glass intaglios, and one-of-a-kind pieces such as micromosaics and antique coins that she will turn into covetable rings, bangles, pendants, and earrings sold at upscale boutiques around the world, including her own in Manhattan and Boyce, Virginia. Bold 19-karat-gold mounts, chunky chains, and hoops encircle and support her extraordinary finds.

The setting where Elizabeth lives with her husband, John Staelin, is equally spectacular. More than thirty years ago, they were plotting a move from New York when they stumbled upon an 1816 Federal-style farmhouse nestled within one hundred acres in Virginia's Shenandoah Valley. They have carefully renovated and shaped both house and garden in a manner that is respectful of its period and place, but that can keep up with the couple's modern-day lifestyle.

Although both Elizabeth's professional and personal pursuits lead her on a never-ending quest to find and create beauty, she delights in bringing home style "souvenirs" to weave into her environment. The garden speaks to her love of Italy, with boxwood parterres, cypress hedges, and oyster-gravel paths, grounded by a Gothic-style conservatory with crisp white outlines. There's also a cutting garden, where perennials reseed at will, along with profuse vegetable beds, a greenhouse for cultivating orchids and cycads, and a coop and space for a dozen chickens to roam. When she's not working, Elizabeth, who is never afraid to get her hands a little dirty, can often be found deadheading the dahlias, harvesting ramps and lettuces, or gathering eggs that her prolific hens have produced.

The fruits of her labor will inevitably make their way to the table, and all the better when that table is shared with others, for entertaining is another of

Elizabeth's many talents. She is not, however, one to host impromptu get-togethers. "For me, so much of the fun is in the planning, overseeing every last detail, putting together the most interesting mix of people, and brainstorming the menu," she says.

On a late-spring afternoon, she sets up a pair of tables on the side porch, where a gentle breeze provides the only air conditioning needed. Guests explore the garden at its peak, glass of wine in hand, before sitting down to a meal that Elizabeth has prepared using the bounty outside her back door. The hens have supplied the main ingredient for a shakshuka (poached eggs in a spicy tomato and pepper sauce); fresh asparagus has been roasted; and rhubarb pulled up just this morning has been transformed into a rhubarb-and-strawberry crisp.

As much as Elizabeth loves to cook, she believes it's the environment and the conversation, rather than the food, that people will remember. Thus, it's no surprise that she puts equal care into the porch decor and table settings; incorporating exuberant tablecloths found in India; chairs painted Charleston green; repoussé silver; colorful glassware; monogrammed linens; and antique Minton china.

"The flowers are like jewels on the table," she says. "I have never formally studied arranging, so my approach is very casual. I keep them loose and work with colors and textures until I get something that is pleasing to me." The effect is indeed memorable, and a cheerful ode to the season and the garden.

RIGHT: The centerpiece of Elizabeth Locke's Virginia garden is a Gothic-style conservatory by Amdega. "I had to close my eyes when I wrote the check, but it has given me more joy than anything I've ever purchased," she says. She can often be found there tending to her orchids, cycads, and palms. PREVIOUS PAGE: Whether for her jewelry, on the table, or in the garden, Elizabeth creates a pretty setting. She sets up a pair of tables on the porch and uses her stash of Chiavari chairs, which she stores in the basement for entertaining. "I spray-painted them Charleston green, which I think is more interesting than the usual gold ballroom chairs," she says. FOLLOWING SPREAD, LEFT PAGE, CLOCKWISE FROM TOP LEFT: Elizabeth prefers plates with minimal decoration, such as her antique Minton china, and lets the pattern come from the tablecloths. A rhubarb-and-strawberry crisp reflects both her cooking skills and her green thumb—she harvested the rhubarb from the garden the morning of the party. RIGHT PAGE: A peony in a vase is as exuberant as the stones in her jewelry designs. Her flower-arranging style is loose.

GARDENING AND ENTERTAINING

The interesting thing about gardening is that you never really get to be an expert—you just keep trying because it's all a question of experience. The more things you try and fail at, the more you learn.

It's fun to share things from my garden. The problem with giving away vegetables around here is that so many people grow their own. They might say "no thanks" to green beans that have taken me an hour to pick, but they'll never turn down a bouquet of dahlias.

I collect antique linens and I must have hundreds of monogrammed napkins. The actual initials don't matter—I pick them for the beauty of the monogram. Now you can find them at antiques shops and flea markets for less than it takes to buy plain ones at a department store. They have a life, and when they get too worn, they go in the ragbag.

If a party is small enough, I almost always do my own cooking. I prep as much in advance as I can.

Place cards add a personal touch, and when you've just been introduced to someone, you can always glance over if you forget his or her name.

HEIRLOOM HOSPITALITY

Chesie Breen
East Hampton, New York

Long a fixture of the New York design world, Chesie Breen leads the living embodiment of a tasteful life. As a marketing guru to Bunny Williams, Cathy Kincaid, David Kleinberg, and Amanda Lindroth, as well as a contributing editor to *House Beautiful,* she promotes the high-style brands of some of the most talented people in the business. She has created a niche for herself in the style hall of fame. And though her own home oozes style, it primarily serves as the repository for values of family, friendship, and fun.

The 1960s ranch, which Chesie and her husband Tommy bought in 2010, is nestled in a vast green lawn, perfect for gymnastics demonstrations by her three daughters, Virginia, Eliza, and Margaret Ivy. "The main reason we moved to East Hampton is that it's really just a small town, and I wanted the girls to grow up with a sense of community," says Chesie "and in a place where you are surrounded by a beautiful environment, with beaches and hiking dunes." Designed by her client the late Greg Jordan, along with Rob Southern, the house displays a timeless preppy-chic vibe.

A childhood spent in Texas and Virginia gave Chesie the firm foundation in Southern traditions she now strives to pass on to her own children. "I think graciousness of living is about making that extra effort when it might be easier to do something else," she says. "What we remember becomes our own traditions and defines our upbringing. It is important for the girls to grow up with good manners as a way to embrace the past and some of

its numerous rituals. I think that is a wonderful inheritance."

When the family entertains, it's all hands on deck, including the smallest. "When we entertain as a family, I don't say, 'Okay, girls, it's time for the party.' We all weigh in and participate in planning, from the menu to the flowers to who will be coming."

For a Mother's Day table setting, the girls incorporate everything heirloom, pulling out Chesie's Haviland wedding china and her great-great-grandmother's dessert plates, arranging flowers, and even inscribing place cards. Each girl contributes flatware from the three Tiffany patterns they have been collecting since birth. "It's a way of being grateful for all that we have," says Chesie. "Hopefully when they're on their own, they'll remember that things shouldn't just sit in a drawer, but rather be used and loved."

RIGHT: Garden roses, hydrangeas, and veronicas fill a scattering of bud vases and silver baby cups as a table centerpiece. Haviland's Vieux Paris Green plates mix with dessert plates inherited from Chesie Breen's great-great-grandmother on the classic Mother's Day luncheon table, with its predominantly pink palette. PREVIOUS PAGE: Drinks are served on the back terrace—prosecco for the adults and raspberry lemonade for the children. The cupcakes are for all. Formal Porthault cocktail napkins paired with a boho John Robshaw tablecloth is a signature Breen pastiche.

ARRANGING AND ENTERTAINING

I like to surprise my three daughters with fresh flowers in their rooms to welcome them home from boarding school, camp, or a trip. I also do this to celebrate a special occasion or accomplishment.

When arranging flowers for the dining table, I combine seasonal fruit, such as plums, figs, and tangerines, with flowers and scatter the fruit, which everyone is free to enjoy, on the table. It's my version of scattered petals.

My favorite hostess gift is a Santa Maria Novella terra-cotta pomegranate. It is a nod to nature that lasts, with a transformative scent.

I mix table linens—my go-to are Leontine Linens mixed with colorful prints from Amanda Lindroth's shop in Palm Beach. And for the bed, I love to mix in printed floral patterns from D. Porthault.

I am a stickler for a handwritten note—and have tried to instill this tradition in my daughters. Each has beautifully engraved stationery from The Printery in Oyster Bay, New York.

ABOVE: Trailing vines of the Gracie wallpaper envelop the dining room, serving as a neutral backdrop for a display of a variety of pink-toned colors.
OPPOSITE, CLOCKWISE FROM TOP LEFT: A purple etched-glass bud vase holding a contrasting dark pink garden rose. Chesie with her daughters, from left, Virginia, Eliza, and Margaret Ivy. A love of flowers extends from the window seat cushions and pillows to their outfits. Chesie's dress is by Shannon McLean. Each daughter has her own silver pattern from Tiffany collected from birth: American Flower, Audubon, and Chrysanthemum. The family uses the girls' flatware all the time, and each daughter takes pride when it's her turn to style the table.

57

IN THE GARDEN

Charlotte Moss
East Hampton, New York

After a hectic week that could easily entail everything from a house installation to a presentation on her latest book to scheming new designs for her various product collections, interior designer Charlotte Moss pulls into the driveway of her second home in East Hampton. In what seems like a New York minute, she kicks off her heels, slips into comfortable clogs, and makes a beeline to the flower room to grab a basket and a pair of clippers. "Before I even go upstairs to unpack my bag, I head straight for the garden," she says. Daisy and Buddy, Charlotte's faithful Cavalier King Charles spaniels, usually scamper alongside, as happy as their mistress to leave city life behind for fragrant English roses and boxwoods, meandering pathways, and plenty of nooks and crannies that demand further investigation. "I stroll the garden to see what's happening and in bloom, and start cutting to make arrangements for the house," says Charlotte.

Not only fresh flowers, but also translated ones flourish throughout the spaces Charlotte creates. They can be as delicate as lilies of the valley rendered in porcelain, as exuberant as a chintz or block-printed fabric enveloping a bedroom, or as refined as a chinoiserie wallpaper of blooming branches in a dining room. "I'm Southern, so flowers run through my veins. I was raised in Virginia by women who had them all around," she says. "It was not necessarily about bringing the outdoors in; it was about making a home feel welcoming and gracious."

However, when Charlotte and her husband, Barry Friedberg, first spotted what they now call Boxwood Terrace, it didn't immediately say "welcome," either in a Southern accent or a Long Island one. It was a somewhat unremarkable spec house on three sprawling acres that featured no landscaping

LEFT: One of the designer's favorite spots to unwind is by the pool in a generously scaled McKinnon and Harris sofa. "I love that moment when you get that blast of sun and the light is fabulous. It's just me, the birds, and the dogs." OPPOSITE: The designer refers to her flower room as her therapy room. "It's where I go to putter, select a vase, listen to music, and power down," she says. PREVIOUS PAGE: On summer afternoons, she often sets a beautiful table on the terrace with her extensive collection of linens and tableware.

to speak of other than a handful of oak trees, a pear allée, and an abundance of arborvitae. "It was the view from the living room window to the backyard that captured me. I imagined what could be," says Charlotte. Given her skill for creating houses that are as livable as they are beautiful, it was no surprise that Charlotte would transform the house into a place that feels like home. But it was the idea of the garden to come—the first of her own—a blank canvas where her artistic touch and passion for detail could really take root, that excited the designer most.

Charlotte enlisted the husband-and-wife team of Lisa Stamm and Dale Booher—she, a garden designer and he, an architect—to guide and assist in bringing her vision to life. Similar to Charlotte's interiors, the garden unfolds in a series of rooms

and moments. "I didn't want one big reveal," she says. "By having a hedge or a walkway or a structure with something behind it, you are constantly making discoveries." Stamm strongly encouraged Charlotte to develop a long-range plan. "It sounds a bit trite, but it's so important, because of the way things grow. Above all, a garden requires patience, something that hasn't always come naturally to me," says Charlotte. More than two decades later, her vision has been firmly established, albeit it's one that has shifted and sharpened its focus, whether due to necessity (Mother Nature sometimes has other plans in store) or the designer's never-ending quest to research and implement new ideas.

"Ultimately, we want to feel that we haven't just arrived at a house, we've arrived at *the* place— where we can really unwind," says Charlotte.

Often the couple has weekend guests in tow, and the designer's love of entertaining slips into gear. On summer afternoons, she'll plan for a buffet-style meal on the terrace. Although the mood may be decidedly low-key and the attire caftans and swimsuit cover-ups, she'll still arrange a dining-room-worthy tablescape with china (often of her own design), colorful linens, and casually composed garden flowers in pieces from her extensive collection of baskets, vases, and jardinieres. "If the flowers look spontaneous and relaxed, they make people relax," says Charlotte.

But just as in the richly layered houses she decorates, nothing in the garden escapes her notice—even an errant dead leaf will be plucked and tossed before she finally sits down with cocktail or iced tea in hand. "I tell everyone in my design office if they're not thinking about the wastepaper basket that goes underneath that beautiful George III writing table, they're missing the boat. The same principle is true in the garden. Paying attention to the smallest of details is what I do."

Boxwood Terrace, Charlotte Moss's weekend getaway in East Hampton, New York, provides a much-needed respite from her fast-paced life as a designer, as well as allows her to create beauty in her downtime with pursuits she is passionate about—gardening, entertaining, and flower arranging.

CHARLOTTE'S PICKS FOR LIVING FLORAL
GARDENING

Patience is rewarded. Gardens can't always be about instant gratification. I remember Lisa Stamm, who collaborated and guided me on our garden, saying, "Let's do climbing hydrangea on the oaks and in five years it will look great." I thought, are you kidding—that long? I eventually realized I was going to have to grow old slowly with some of those trees. Now it has been more than twenty years, and the climbing hydrangea rocks on.

Stylistic tastes, like the garden, evolve. In the beginning, I wanted that perfect English herbaceous border—my Gertrude Jekyll moment—with undulating color and a riot of blooms. The maintenance made me crazy. As time went by, I wanted to simplify my life, and the more gardens I saw, the more I appreciated the glory of green, and what could be done in shaping it and the architecture of the garden.

Everything doesn't have to be a lifelong commitment. Change can happen in pots. It doesn't have to happen in the ground. A cluster of containers in the right place allows me so much freedom to experiment with color, texture, and height.

ABOVE: Charlotte is continually inspired to bring ideas from her travels home. She was so enchanted with the willow structures at France's Prieuré Notre-Dame d'Orsan that she asked the head gardener, Gilles Guillot, to create similar features in her own garden, including what she calls the hickory pavilion. OPPOSITE, CLOCKWISE FROM TOP LEFT: A porcelain basket holds roses from the garden. "When the roses are in bloom, there's a lot of pink in the garden," says Charlotte, who finds relaxation in tending them and clipping blossoms for arrangements. A Chinese fretwork piece that once belonged to Bunny Mellon is filled with potted ferns and large-leaf begonias.

FALL

AUTUMN ALFRESCO

Ashley Whittaker
Millbrook, New York

Designer Ashley Whittaker is known for her fresh interpretations of classical styles, mingling antiques and bold palettes in rooms that are both lively and livable. From her office and pied-à-terre in Manhattan, she spends the week creating homes for other people's experiences, but on weekends, it's off to her heart's home in Millbrook, New York. "I appreciate and get so much energy from the bustle of the city, but I absolutely love living in the country," says Ashley. She and her husband, Andrew Spence, chose it as the perfect place to raise a family, with its rare mix of sophistication and natural beauty. And it's there that she entertains friends, indoors when the climate demands but outside whenever possible.

On a glorious fall afternoon, she invited friends for an autumnal feast amidst the best of Hudson River Valley glory. A nearby dressage farm owned by friends provided the setting for an alfresco feast and bonfire. A perfect, crisp fall day provided the backdrop for cocktails served from a former Army ammunition trailer–turned–mobile bar, as well as a seated dinner around a table that would be impressive in any glamorous dining room. With her keen eye for detail, and a master's confidence in mixing materials, Ashley assembled a table setting emblematic of her original style. "For me, it's about contrasts," she says. "I want a table to be collected with special things, using the formal with the informal, and a mix of textures, periods, and color. A room should feel the same way."

Faux bois china and staghorn flatware reflect the horse-loving setting, elevated from the usual outdoor ware and all the more luxurious for its whimsical use under the fall foliage. A tablecloth instantly created the feeling

of a room, and Ashley's use of a botanical print is proof that a natural print holds its own in the great outdoors. A centerpiece uses the foliage of the season to embellish the scenery without attempting to upstage it. Rusty red leaves echo the hue of the red wine filling the goblets, making subtle reference to the harvest season.

One of Ashley's great design skills is inserting just the right note of rusticity into a city room. In a happy bit of irony, the inverse of that skill also appears to be true. She is equally adept at bringing uptown elegance to dinner on a farm. And she finds the effort entirely worthwhile. "Fall is a magical time in Millbrook," she says. "It's definitely something to celebrate."

RIGHT: A former U.S. Army ammunition trailer now serves as designer Ashley Whittaker's party wagon for polo tailgates, horse shows, and dinner parties. Flowers and greenery from the property adorn the improvised outdoor dining room. PREVIOUS PAGE: For a party at Roseview Farms, Ashley uses green and brown decorative elements in a rustic yet refined table setting anchored by a favorite botanical fabric from Jasper by Michael S. Smith. FOLLOWING SPREAD, LEFT PAGE, CLOCKWISE FROM TOP LEFT: Ashley and friends linger close to the bonfire on a cool afternoon. Cocktails are served from the party wagon's mobile bar, with a wood ice bucket filled with wild flowers, grasses, and greenery from the property as the perfect rustic accent. *Faux bois* china and naturally shed staghorn flatware add organic touches to the table. RIGHT PAGE: The autumnal chill in the air calls for comfort food, like individual chicken potpies, which Ashley sources from Babette's Kitchen in Millbrook.

ASHLEY'S PICKS FOR LIVING FLORAL

DECORATING AND ARRANGING

Rooms should feel as if they have evolved over time. That is also true for tablescapes and the materials that go into them. I've collected things over the years that resonate with me.

In a rustic setting outside, I'll incorporate interior elements that give some formality to the table, such as a chintz tablecloth. My chairs and table are brought from home. The effort makes guests feel special.

I like to include a bit of the unexpected. A party wagon serves a practical function to get things to a remote "dining room," and provides decorative interest that feels at home in a horse-farm setting. People love gathering around it to fix their plates and cocktails.

I love unorchestrated flower arrangements, and I'm a huge collector of anything that could be used for them. I'm drawn to repurposed vessels, such as antique biscuit boxes, silver pitchers, and white or cream containers, because they make everything pop and frame the arrangement.

The things that make an interior interesting also apply to table settings and flowers: texture, color, and mixing periods and styles. I'll use formal linens with Adirondack chairs or staghorn flatware with contemporary drinking glasses from CB2.

Dishes like catered chicken potpies are perfect for transporting to an outdoor venue, because I can bring them out piping hot and they'll be warm when we sit down.

AT THE CHEF'S TABLE

Pardis and Frank Stitt
Birmingham, Alabama

C ome on in—we're so glad you're here," offers Pardis Stitt, with a gracious and engaging smile. It's a kind of welcome that Birmingham locals and food lovers from all over have come to appreciate when they flock to any of the four restaurants she owns with her husband, Frank, the much-lauded chef who put Birmingham on the culinary map more than thirty years ago with Highlands Bar & Grill. When he opened his first restaurant, the city was primarily dominated by barbecue joints, meat-and-threes, and the kind of predictable fare served in country-club dining rooms. Frank shook up the culinary landscape by elevating Southern ingredients with classic French techniques and flavor combinations that were sophisticated, without any hint of pretension. Using what was fresh and locally sourced, the restaurant had a farm-to-table sensibility long before it was the hottest trend on everyone's lips. Word of mouth about what was emerging from Highlands' kitchen soon spread beyond Birmingham's borders, as one bite of his baked grits doused in a buttery Parmesan sauce and garnished with wild mushrooms and country ham could instantly convert even the most skeptical Northerner.

About fifteen years ago, Pardis and Frank began plotting to find a farm of their own. "We wanted a place that would not only provide us with ingredients for the restaurants, but that would also be a laboratory of learning," explains Frank. They purchased what they would name Paradise Farm, a fifty-five-acre property (with an additional fifteen acres that surround their farmhouse just down the road), and now, several days a week, you can find one of the Stitts or a member of the kitchen staff working alongside the farm's caretakers to plant, tend, and harvest the herbs, tomatoes, beans, lettuces, roses, nasturtiums, and such. "Being a part of the process changes you," says Frank. "We've always

appreciated and continue to support our area farmers, but when you're actually out there doing the work, you're likely to be less wasteful and much more respectful of what they do and what you're cooking with."

The farm also yields gorgeous blooms for the tables in the farmhouse and in town at the restaurants, including roses, dahlias, and nasturtiums, and Stitts' daughter's summer wedding on the farm was filled with locally grown blooms, grasses, and vines.

Clearly both the Stitts are natural-born hosts, and that goes for their days off, too. As friends arrive at the farmhouse for perhaps the most coveted "reservation" of all—an invitation for a relaxed Sunday afternoon repast—they're greeted at the front door by Pardis with a tray of refreshing drinks in hand, and Fiona, the couple's amiable dog, who is by her side.

Pardis has laid a casual, but thoughtfully composed table setting. Just as many of the meal's components will come from the garden, so do the flowers. "I use things that we grow with intention, such as roses or hydrangeas, but I'll also walk around the property and gather what catches my eye. Sometimes I don't know the names, or they might even be weeds, but I'll just think they're pretty and bring them in," says Pardis. "As long as they don't have a strong scent that will interfere with the food," adds Frank, with the seasoned perspective of a chef, of course. She often chooses unexpected vessels, rather than traditional vases. Today she has pulled out ceramic soup bowls for several low arrangements that parade down the table. Handwritten menu cards announce the delectable meal to come,

RIGHT: The bounty of Pardis and Frank Stitt's farm not only provides sustenance, but also decoration. On the porch, cattails, crowder peas, beans, and figs are arranged in pitchers and urns. An antique silver caddy cools bottles of rosé. PREVIOUS PAGE: On a Sunday afternoon, the couple gathers friends around the table to partake in the flavors of the season, many of which have been harvested from Paradise Farm, their property in Harpersville, Alabama.

and antique silver mingles with striped linens and French bistro glasses, much of which has been collected with the help of Patrick Dunne, a friend and the proprietor of Lucullus, a New Orleans shop that specializes in culinary antiques.

"I'm a planner, a put-it-on-paper kind of person," says Pardis. "I like the platters labeled with what will go on them, and as much done beforehand as we can. Frank is about à la minute. So we come at things a bit differently, but ultimately make it work." The friends who have gathered around the table, not to mention anyone who has dined at their restaurants, would enthusiastically agree. From the first taste of a juicy fig paired with prosciutto to the last spoonful of cantaloupe sorbet, the Stitts make it work beautifully, indeed.

ABOVE: "I love using unexpected containers as vases," says Pardis, who chooses ceramic soup bowls for garden flowers on the table. OPPOSITE, CLOCKWISE FROM TOP LEFT: Pardis, Frank, and their beloved dog, Fiona, enjoy a quiet moment in the kitchen. When the party's over, Pardis will send everyone home with a jar of honey from the farm's beehives. "One of the most amazing things I've ever eaten was a ripe melon and prosciutto di Parma in Venice. No matter how fancy you get you can't improve upon that," says Frank. His guests might disagree after sampling his platter of figs from Paradise Farm, prosciutto, Chilton County peaches, and goat cheese from nearby Stone Hollow Farmstead.

ENTERTAINING AND ARRANGING

Even when we're entertaining casually, we often have a progression of courses versus serving everything family-style or all at once. The pacing is something I really appreciate. Not as many people take the trouble to do that as they might have twenty or thirty years ago.

I usually prefer food to be on a white or off-white plate, as I don't want the dinnerware to compete with what's being served. The colors of a ratatouille or the peaches, figs, and walnuts—those are the things that I want to notice.

Pardis and I love things with a history or story, such as eighteenth-century silver or the French linens that have come to us through Patrick Dunne at Lucullus in New Orleans. They have soul and authenticity to them.

One rule of thumb for me is that there be no fragrant flowers on the table, or even in the same room as the food. I want nothing to compete with the delectable smells and tastes of the food. So we usually cut things from the field like grasses or pods, and even use fruits as table decor.

79

VINTAGE STYLE IN BLOOM

Schuyler Samperton
Los Angeles, California

Between her father, architect Jack Samperton, and her mother, Novella, who was one of Washington, D.C.'s best-dressed women in the 1970s, Schuyler Samperton has a strong style pedigree. But she's carved her own design niche with homes for celebrity clients that exude freewheeling West Coast glamour spiced with global flavors. A passion for vintage textiles permeates her work, with suzanis and period chintz mixed in a casual way that speaks of a world traveler versed in many languages of style.

"My mother never did what everyone else was doing," says Schuyler, "and she instilled in me the importance of originality. Dad designed our house, but it was Mom who decorated it with gray flannel–covered sofas, fur rugs, and a not entirely practical but nonetheless great-looking Don Drumm coffee table. And we always had flowers in the house. Mom spent a lot of time on that detail."

"Today, I personally gravitate to antiques, color, and pattern, but Mom gave me a willingness to take chances with how I mix and layer more traditional things," she says. During a stint working for Michael Smith, the Los Angeles designer who decorated the Obama White House, Schuyler was tasked with managing projects and, significantly, styling clients' houses with flowers for photo shoots. "I loved accessorizing and working with floral designers to figure out how to make a room look its most beautiful. Michael had very specific ideas in terms of the varieties of flowers he wanted, their color and height, and what sort of container should be used."

Since opening her own firm in 2003, Schuyler has formed a collaboration with floral designer Louesa Roebuck, who appears to inhabit the same design sphere. Louesa does what she calls "wild harvesting," where she goes to abandoned lots and fields to gather branches, wild flowers, garden roses, and such. Her arrangements reflect that natural feel. For example, magnolia branches retain the curve they had on the tree. She doesn't force the shapes.

Floral motifs abound in Schuyler's designed rooms, from a de Gournay chinoiserie wallpaper in actor Yeardley Smith's dining room to model Carolyn Murphy's dreamy vintage floral fabrics that complement her bohemian, country style. "I never want anything I decorate to feel unapproachable or precious," she says. "It's important to me that my works create a comfortable environment that feels like home. But whether it's a floral wallpaper, vintage textile, or fresh arrangement, I will always love designing with flowers."

RIGHT: Flowers, both the fresh variety and artistic interpretations, abound in designer Schuyler Samperton's Los Angeles living room. The floral painting on wood was inherited from her parents. Botanical motifs dominate her global assortment of vintage pillows. PREVIOUS PAGE: In Schuyler's West Hollywood living room, shades of green are the unifying theme tying together textiles, art, and collections. The magnolia on the vine was provided by floral designer Louesa Roebuck. FOLLOWING SPREAD, LEFT PAGE, CLOCKWISE FROM TOP LEFT: Schuyler's passion for flowers is revealed in her idea board of photos tacked to her bathroom wall, as well as the embroidered hand towels on display. Schuyler embraces the cool of autumn seated on her plant-filled porch. For actor Yeardley Smith's dining room, Schuyler chose a de Gournay blue-painted chinoiserie wallpaper to reflect the homeowner's love of natural motifs. RIGHT PAGE: Seemingly spilling over, a loose gathering of magnolia branches picks up the white sprigs of flowers on the hand-painted Bloomsbury-inspired patterned wallpaper in Schuyler's dining room.

SCHUYLER'S PICKS FOR LIVING FLORAL
DECORATING AND ARRANGING

What I've embraced from my mom is the way she combined things—leather, suede, feathers, fur, velvet, tall boots, huge wide-brimmed hats, scarves, and jeweled belts. That's my approach with flowers too. I like mixing textures in plant material, and high and low style like fancy David Austin roses with some humble, foraged wild asters.

Flowers on my bedside table may be floating gardenias, garden roses, sweet peas—anything that has a lovely scent.

My favorite floral-related art are Oberto Gili's huge bloom photos, and Lawrence Alma-Tadema's paintings of glorious swags, potted oleander, and orchids.

THE GRACIOUS HOST

James Carter
Birmingham, Alabama

Like many design professionals, Birmingham architect James Carter creates exquisite homes for others but was slow to get around to his own house. For years, he inhabited temporary quarters that never really reflected his tastes and talents. The wait was worth it, however, when he finally built his dream house and, in 2017, was able to unpack the treasures he'd accumulated over years of study and travel.

"For three years, I lived in a teardown on the property where I eventually built this house," he says. "It was basically a storage shed and I never had people over." When his new house was finished, one of the most gratifying prospects was his newfound ability to repay the hospitality of friends who'd entertained him during the previous years. On a recent fall weekend, with the Antiques at The Gardens show drawing many of his friends to Birmingham, James invited a group of locals and out-of-towners for brunch, toasting the conclusion of a weekend of creative inspiration.

"To me, brunch can be an elegant way to entertain. The food may be simple but it has to be delicious. I don't cook but I know people who do it really well. I served a main course of quiche, prepared from Thomas Keller's recipe, along with candied bacon, and a salad. Good wine is important," says James, "but it's really about the people, and they want to chat." Rather than seating his guests around a formal table, a buffet allowed for ease of eating while catching up.

Growing up in Monroeville, Alabama, home to Harper Lee, James was exposed to the kind of small-town entertaining where multiple generations gathered frequently and expert hostesses set a tone of gracious welcome. "My grandmothers ran really nice homes and threw beautiful family dinners,"

says James. "I've always admired people who can do that." A set of antique Spode neoclassical china, reflecting James's love of English Regency style, brought his point of view to the meal. "I am especially focused on the years between 1790 and 1830," he says. The house is full of accents such as an Egyptian Revival urn, a Regency tea caddy, and antique Wedgwood adorning the shelves and surfaces. Architectural watercolors and Italian gouaches round out his collection, gathered in his travels and framed as his mood suits.

Since guests were given free rein to explore his colorful, antiques-filled rooms, friend and floral designer Sybil Sylvester positioned spectacular arrangements of fall blooms all over the house. Dahlias, persimmon branches, and greenery from the yard reflected the orange and red hues James favors, colors that frequently appear in classic ceramics and artwork. Perched on surfaces in every room, they served as welcoming signposts of hospitality. "I love the idea of doing something extra for friends," he says. "After many years of living in a shoebox, it's such a pleasure to share my home with them."

JAMES'S PICKS FOR LIVING FLORAL
ENTERTAINING

Don't invite so many people that you don't have a chance to talk to everyone. It's better to have several smaller parties than one big "cattle call."

Keep the menu simple but delicious, especially if you're a novice cook like me.

Most people I know go to parties to socialize—not to eat. Leave the gourmet cooking to great chefs.

If your budget allows, hire some help in the kitchen and for cleanup. If you're a little short, don't be proud—ask your friends for help. But try not to make it a habit.

All of my friends who know flowers tell me to only use flowers from the garden. I have loosely interpreted that to include ones that could have come from the garden. So when doing the flowers myself, I will glean from my garden but also head to the wholesaler, always keeping in mind that I'm not entering a flower show, and can use simpler—or should I say, "humbler"—varieties.

ABOVE: In the bedroom of architect James Carter's dream home in Birmingham, Alabama, against walls painted a pine-leaf green, floral designer Sybil Sylvester fashioned an arrangement of marigolds, black-eyed Susans, white zinnias, and pyracantha for a dash of contrast. OPPOSITE, CLOCKWISE FROM TOP LEFT: In an upstairs landing, an arrangement of peegee hydrangeas, dahlias, marigolds, wild grasses, pumpkin tree, and red sage rewards a climb up the stairs. James enjoys the ability to host friends in his home. In the lofty screened porch, Sybil fashioned a towering arrangement to fill the space with pampas grass, leucothoes, elaeagnuses, 'Little Gem' magnolias, sea oats, maple leaves, peegee hydrangeas, and wild grasses.

FRIENDS AND FAMILY FEAST

Wendy Wurtzburger
Philadelphia, Pennsylvania

Wendy Wurtzburger suffers the affliction shared by many design professionals—her discerning eye never rests, finding opportunities for stylish expression everywhere. As chief merchandising and design officer for Anthropologie, focused mainly on the tabletop category, Wendy traveled the world searching for fresh finds for the global retail brand. These days, in addition to her work as a retail consultant, she and partner Mitzi Wong design their own line, Roar + Rabbit, for West Elm.

Wendy and her husband, Chris Bentley, live in a charming 1840s farmhouse in Philadelphia on four and a half acres abutting the Wissahickon Valley Park. "The house and gardens are oriented toward the park," says Wendy. "With the outdoor fireplaces, it's an all-seasons house for entertaining."

Recently, Wendy and Chris hosted a harvest dinner for friends and enlisted a tribe of talented young people to help with the components. Kristen Jas Vietty, a grower and floral designer whom Wendy befriended at her local farmer's market, agreed to handle floral arrangements. She arrived with buckets of blooms but also indulged in her passion for foraging, collecting leaves and faded autumnal blooms from the gardens. By party time, a lavish runner of dahlias, hydrangeas, persimmons, pomegranates, and lady apples extended from one end of the dining table to the other, and seasonal floral accents adorned every available surface.

For the menu, based on fruits and vegetables from their garden, the couple enlisted their son Robin, a culinary school graduate who worked at The Finch in Brooklyn, and their friends' daughter, Lidey Heuck. Lidey,

who works for Ina Garten in East Hampton, New York, set about concocting a pear cake for dessert, while Robin braised pork for a savory main dish. Another son, Charlie, who is a graphic designer, stoked the outdoor pizza oven to roast clams for the feast. Among the invited guests were Brian Foster and Ernie Sesskin, who made the outdoor dining table. Walter and Katy Palmer, who own a distillery, contributed their craft Liberty Gin for the special cocktail.

Wendy's restless and unerring eye for style focused on the table, which she set with a mixture of inherited heirloom china and treasures from her globe-trotting adventures. "I inherited a ridiculous amount of old things from family," she says. "But I do believe in using the good stuff every day." Her grandmother's Copenhagen china mingled with pretty yellow wineglasses she sourced during her years at Anthropologie. Napkins she found on a recent jaunt to Guatemala brought a note of that brave mix to the setting. Soup was served in tiny terra-cotta pitchers she found on the same trip.

As Wendy and Chris gathered with their children and friends around their splendid outdoor table, the rustic setting belied the sophistication of the talents contributing to the gathering. "I love the idea of nature meets glamour, country meets city," says Wendy.

ABOVE: Wendy Wurtzburger lives in an 1840s farmhouse, which was reinvented as a French Second Empire–style house in the 1890s, in the Mount Aerie neighborhood of urban Philadelphia's rare bucolic oasis. Wendy and her husband, Chris Bentley, enjoy sharing their place with friends. Gourds from the garden add seasonal color and sculptural impact. OPPOSITE: An arrangement of scabiosas, gomphrena, perilla, and dahlias for a fall party adorns a serving table, which rests on a base made from an upturned metal garbage can. PREVIOUS PAGE: A blush-pink arrangement of hydrangeas, gomphrena, scabiosas, dahlias, and perilla takes a fresh approach to fall color.

WENDY'S PICKS FOR LIVING FLORAL
ENTERTAINING AND ARRANGING

If you own a multitude of different china patterns, mix them all and it works better than trying to pick out a couple that match exactly. It's also more interesting. Floral and botanical prints work really well, especially when dining alfresco. It's as if they're trumpeting the setting.

Fruit and herbs from the garden make for an easy, festive garnish.

Most people shy away from dried florals, but dried leaves, pods, and blooms—especially if foraged from the property—look just right in the fall, and pair well with informal bohemian flower arrangements.

Mixed flower arrangements can be visually tied into the surroundings by using plant materials found on the property like the leaves of Boston ivy that echo the climbing ivy on a trellis.

ABOVE: On the bar table, an arrangement of dahlias and hydrangeas mingled with nandina berries foraged from Wendy's garden complements the signature pear cocktail with Liberty Gin and pear liqueur. A textile from Guatemala provides a burst of color on the table beneath a mirror reflecting the dramatic scenery. OPPOSITE, CLOCKWISE FROM TOP LEFT: Wendy loves to add nasturtiums from her kitchen garden to salads. Under the pergola, Wendy puts finishing touches on the table centerpiece; friends Brian Foster and Ernie Sesskin built the outdoor dining table from a felled tree on the property, while Wendy appreciates the industrial chairs for their contrast with the pretty stone terrace. Chef Lidey Heuck baked the wow-worthy pear and hazelnut cake for dessert.

Kristen Jas Vietty of Lunaria Gardens fashioned a floral runner down the center of the table incorporating potted coral bells, dahlias, celosias, nasturtiums, Fuyu persimmons, pomegranates, and greenery. A rustic linen runner sets off the colorful centerpiece. Napkins that Wendy found on a recent trip to Guatemala mix comfortably with china she inherited from her grandmother.

WINTER

EXPERT ENTERTAINING

Alex Hitz
Los Angeles, California

I f you're lucky enough to snag an invitation to chef, cookbook author, and master entertainer Alex Hitz's Christmas Eve party for friends, reply yes. For his annual dinner for forty at his Los Angeles home, Alex leaves no detail to chance. "My entertaining philosophy: Serve dinner on time. Never let the wine flow like glue. Make sure the food is impeccable, simple, and indulgent. And never, ever run out of it."

An Atlanta native, Alex learned his hosting skills from his mother, Caroline, who married Robert Shaw, famed conductor of the Atlanta Symphony, and "entertained constantly," he says. From her he learned to manage the unpredictable cocktail hour. "Forty-five minutes is plenty for cocktails," he says. "My party begins at 7:30 p.m. and I'll pass Champagne and sparkling water. If guests desire something even stronger, my homemade eggnog is decadent and lethal."

At the holidays, Alex sets the table with ornate china, gleaming silver, and splashes of red. "I unapologetically go for red," he says, "and what's on the table reflects my sense of tradition, style, and family history. I've been fortunate to inherit some fine tableware, and I'm a firm believer in using the good stuff as often as possible." A florist friend, David Jones, prepared centerpieces of carnations in three shades of red, which deliver a big impact for a low sticker price. Bowls of crimson apples center other tables, surrounded by a grove of metallic gold trees Alex picked up for a song.

Most of all, Alex advises remaining calm. "Things will happen," he says. "A Baccarat glass will surely get broken. What are you going to do? The more stressed-out you are, the more uncomfortable your guests are going to be. A party is like a watch. You just have to wind it up, and then let it go."

LEFT: Alex Hitz's Christmas Eve party for friends is an elegant affair. Golden fir trees surround a silver bowl mounded with apples for a simple but luxurious centerpiece. PREVIOUS PAGE: Arrangements of three shades of carnations march down the center of the long table, which is dressed with silver candlesticks and monogrammed linens. FOLLOWING SPREAD, LEFT PAGE, CLOCKWISE FROM TOP LEFT: Floral designer David Jones massed carnations in various shades of red in antique silver holloware, like this sterling Cartier tureen. With all the party preparations complete, the host checks his look. Alex sets a round table with Royal Crown Derby Kings Imari china and Francis I flatware, and a centerpiece of red apples. RIGHT PAGE: Family silver, monogrammed linens, and festive flowers add a layer of tradition and shimmer to the Christmas Eve soirée.

ALEX'S PICKS FOR LIVING FLORAL
DECORATING AND ENTERTAINING

A party is theater. It's all about timing and the components that go into the event.

You and your guests are the stars of the show. Decor should be attractive and tasteful but not a distraction. A palm frond in a glass cylinder is simple and chic.

Nothing kills a mood faster than a room lit for surgery. I always dim, dim, dim, and then use tapers and votives everywhere.

Don't skimp on props. I always want fresh flowers, and if I'm in California, there's always something gorgeous blooming outside. It is helpful for me, who prepares the dinner, to have someone else arrange the flowers. Professionals are divine, but good friends who call ahead to say they're bringing a centerpiece, asking your color scheme, are even better.

Limit your extras—no hors d'oeuvres. Why ruin the main event? How many times have you overindulged in deliciously rich canapés and then not appreciated the dinner? And don't feel as though you have to provide a party favor—you've planned, cooked, decorated, sent beautiful invitations, created a playlist (or enlisted your talented friend to play the piano), and opened your home to a cast of several. That's a gracious plenty.

HOLIDAY WREATH-MAKING PARTY

Mindy Rice
Santa Barbara, California

Event planner and floral designer Mindy Rice comes by her talents naturally. Her grandmother was a couture fashion designer and worked with famed costume designer Edith Head. Her mother set a tone of elevated style that manifests in Mindy's current work. "My mom always put an importance on friends, family, entertaining, and home," she says. "We never sat down to a mediocre meal on a mediocre table. It was always beautiful, and it changed with every season. I wasn't really even aware of the artistry around me then. But clearly, it soaked in."

While studying at the Fashion Institute of Design and Merchandising in Los Angeles, Mindy began doing window displays for local businesses. By age seventeen, she had undertaken her first wedding and says, "It just snowballed from there. The most important element of entertaining is to have a relaxed host or hostess. If you're preoccupied or stressed, it will impact your guests. Don't fret over the little things."

For floral designers and wedding planners, summers are an incessant whirl of parties to orchestrate, months in the planning and intense in execution. But in the off-season, Mindy takes advantage of the lull to flex her entertaining muscles and gather friends at a scenic ranch to celebrate the Christmas season. Her annual wreath-making party combines socializing, fresh air, and creativity that pays off in a gorgeous holiday decoration. "Weddings are work," she says, "but wreath-making is just fun."

Two dozen friends, from investment bankers to landscape architects, gather at the rustic Roblar Ranch in the Santa Ynez Valley, where they are promptly

MINDY'S PICKS FOR LIVING FLORAL
ARRANGING

In a pinch, use collections of stones, feathers, jars, and wooden boxes to create beautiful tablescapes. Add snippets of herbs or single flowers in goblets down the center.

When designing for a farm-to-table meal with lots of platters or for a narrow table where space is limited, I use individual vases set in front of each guest or a posy of fragrant blooms set at each napkin.

For an easy centerpiece, fill a unique vessel with dramatic, loose tree branches, and pair it with a bowl filled with a seasonal harvest, such as pinecones, persimmons, apples, and acorns.

Texture plays a major role in our arrangements. The use of tendrils, lichen, twigs, rocks, acorns, and even exposed roots adds interesting and unexpected details that help complete the design.

ABOVE: Mindy Rice uses a barn of the former cattle ranch, built in the 1930s, for a wreath-making event. A friend shows off the result of her own wreath-making effort. OPPOSITE, CLOCKWISE FROM TOP LEFT: Mindy's Nubian goat, Wally, explores the barn where the guests find wreath-making workstations—burlap-covered tables—prepared for them. Mindy adds a finishing touch to the doorway of her barn with a cluster of greenery. She supplies her guests with butcher aprons, wire wreath forms, pruning shears, and Ohana clippers. PREVIOUS PAGE: Bundles of roses are hung upside down two weeks before the party and make a colorful addition to the barn. Mindy forages the property for materials like the lemon branches to incorporate into the wreath designs.

handed glasses of Champagne. "I like to make sure everybody has something in their hands and gets busy immediately," she says. "It can be eating, drinking, or creating. The party will come to life immediately." Mindy has set up workstations in the clapboard barn from the 1930s. Antique buckets filled with olive branches, pinecones, moss, and dried flowers decorate the barn, and each guest's station is marked with a jaunty feed bag emblazoned with her name and equipped with pruning shears, clippers, and wire wreath forms.

Guests are encouraged to forage from their own yards for materials to add to the mix. "One of my friends has a beautiful succulent garden, one has a walnut farm and gilds her walnuts and

gorgeous magnolia, and another brings bay leaves and dried hydrangeas," she says. Mindy delivers a brief tutorial on wreath-making but tries to let guests direct their own efforts: "Otherwise the wreaths will all look the same."

In lieu of a seated lunch, Mindy serves platters of sandwiches that guests recognize from year to year: curried chicken sandwiches, her mother's egg salad on a pretzel roll, and grilled winter vegetables on ciabatta, each wrapped in waxed paper. Cranberry-colored crystal dishes and stemware add a note of formality and are a nod to the season. By the end of the afternoon, each guest has a finished wreath to take home, which will dry and keep throughout the extended holiday season.

ABOVE: A watering can filled with berries, cotton branches, and greenery gathered from the ranch and guests' yards reflects the season. Materials like wheat weaves and cotton branches bring a rustic note of farm life to the mix. "The nice thing about winter," Mindy says, "is that anything still on the trees is going to dry well." OPPOSITE, TOP LEFT: Calligraphed place cards tied to feed bags mark each guest's station. TOP RIGHT: A constant supply of food and drink keeps guests' energy from flagging.

SETTING THE SCENE

Bryan Batt
New Orleans, Louisiana

Bryan Batt puts on a good show—on screen, on stage, and at home. A veteran of the New York theater scene, he has appeared in a number of Broadway productions, among them *Beauty and the Beast* and *Cats,* but perhaps he remains best known for his television role as Salvatore Romano, the ad agency's art director in AMC's retro-stylish hit series *Mad Men.* He is also an accomplished author, designer, and shop owner. Batt was born and bred in New Orleans, a city known for both its character and its cast of characters. However, Bryan prefers to stay out of the spotlight when entertaining at home, hosting get-togethers to celebrate anything, everything, or nothing at all. To kick off the awards season, he plans a small but chic gathering with all the glamour and glitz of Hollywood.

Against the lush backdrop of the late-nineteenth-century raised Creole cottage that he shares with his spouse Tom Cianfichi, Bryan sets the stage for an intimate evening of stargazing over drinks and dinner with friends. The luminous palette of gold, silver, and bronze, inspired by the precious metal (and highly coveted) statues and orbs awarded over the course of the season, casts a glow on the festivities. Resting on the custom travertine-topped dining table, Tiffany sterling flatware and vintage Steuben crystal hobnob with sleek faux-lizard chargers, chunky earthenware plates glazed in gold, and stained-glass votives from Hazelnut, the chic Magazine Street design emporium Bryan and Tom founded in 2003. As the final gilded touch, oversize linen napkins in a gold damask print fan out of feather-shaped beaded napkin rings.

However, Bryan believes that even a little gilt and sparkle can't upstage the natural beauty of flowers. Arrangements of garden roses, spray roses, anemones,

waxflowers, and hypericum—in shades of golden yellow, pearly white, and Champagne pink—mingle with straight-from-the-garden greenery, including magnolia branches, seeded eucalyptus, and leucadendrons.

The host won't get rattled if the party goes a little off script, as he knows that a wine spill or a chipped glass is bound to happen. And he is never afraid to "break out the good stuff," as he calls it. "A dear family friend gave me a silver mint julep cup for each one of my opening night performances," Bryan says. "Each cup is engraved with the name of the show and the date. They are among my most cherished pieces but are also among my most frequently used. Never save things for a fancy or more special occasion, because there is no occasion more worthy than the gathering of great friends."

RIGHT: To kick off the awards season, actor and designer Bryan Batt holds a small chic gathering in his New Orleans home. Lighting makes or breaks the scene. In the dining room, a Baccarat chandelier is accompanied by a pair of trompe l'oeil theater props that were hardwired for use as wall sconces. Arrangements of garden roses, spray roses, waxflowers, and hypericum act as colorful counterpoints for straight-from-the-garden greenery, including magnolia branches, seeded eucalyptus, and leucadendrons. PREVIOUS PAGE: An antique Sumatran headdress, a vintage candlestick lamp, and an arrangement of roses and anemones bring drama to a clean-lined console. FOLLOWING SPREAD, LEFT PAGE: Bryan loves using old things in new ways, including this eighteenth-century French armoire repurposed as a wet bar. RIGHT PAGE, CLOCKWISE FROM TOP LEFT: A terra-cotta bust of "screaming Bacchus" calls guests to a tray of Champagne. Bryan uses both flutes and coupes to give guests options, and because they look better corralled on the tray—less coordinated and more collected. Bryan strikes a pose on the second-story porch of his home. On the dining room table, large arrangements overflow from trophy-shaped crystal vases, while silver mint julep cups coddle smaller, tighter mounds of blossoms.

BRYAN'S PICKS FOR LIVING FLORAL

ENTERTAINING

Make a grand entrance. But if you're a guest, don't arrive at the party too early or too late.

Conquer entertaining fright. Don't sweat the small stuff. Relax and have fun hosting.

Know your role. Do what you do best, and cast the rest. To put it bluntly, if you're not a cook, hire a caterer.

Be your best. Offer a festive "mocktail" for the designated drivers, mamas-in-the-making, and other souls not imbibing.

No regrets—accidents happen. Red wine will inevitably spill. Think of a stain as a "parting gift" from a guest who had a really good time.

CHRISTMAS CHEER

Rebecca Vizard
St. Joseph, Louisiana

During the holidays, Rebecca Vizard's home hums with the sound of good music, the tinkle of ice in cocktail glasses, the clatter of pots and pans in the kitchen, and lots of laughter. "Family and friends always love to gather here," says Rebecca, speaking of Locustland, the house where she and her husband, Michael, live in St. Joseph, Louisiana, a tiny town carved in the delta of the Mississippi River.

Rebecca adores a good story. Indeed, she can take something as ordinary as directions to her house, located in what she calls "the middle of nowhere," and craft a yarn with as many twists as the back roads that lead you there. While she has written a book, pen and paper are not her usual tools for creating drama; rather it's the antique textiles, embroidery, and trims she gives new life to the exquisite pillows she designs and sells to decorators and collectors. And of course, most of these exquisite embellishments are of a botanical nature.

Rebecca remembers when the last place she wanted to settle down was St. Joseph, where she grew up. She dreamed of pursuing an artistic path in Paris or Manhattan—or virtually any place that had more than one traffic light. But after a stint in New Orleans for college at Tulane University and after marrying and starting a family, the prodigal daughter returned. Her father convinced Michael to succeed him in running the hometown bank.

Little did she realize back then that she was sowing the seeds for the venture that would become B. Viz Design. "I couldn't even buy thread in town," she says. But as she was decorating houses for clients and friends who lived in much bigger cities, she realized she still couldn't find the kind of interesting pillows she wanted for her projects, not even in her nirvana of New York. "Everything was so overly trimmed and fussy at the time," she says.

LEFT AND PREVIOUS PAGE: Stockings are a beloved tradition at Christmastime, particularly in Rebecca Vizard's house, where they are works of art made with vintage fabrics and trims she finds all over the world. Large ones are hung on the mantel, while elf-size ones hold treats for guests. Rebecca wraps gifts with marbleized papers and tops them off with small stockings. OPPOSITE: She also loves to decorate for the holidays with natural materials such as flowers, greenery, and citrus. In the breakfast room, she bedecks the chandelier with cedar, ribbon, and glittery stars.

She decided to make them herself, learning all she could about the nuances, history, and craftsmanship of antique textiles and embroidery decoration. Now she sources burnished metallic trims; ecclesiastical vestments; and antique Fortuny, suzani, and tapestry fabrics while traveling through the French and Italian countryside, Turkey, South America, and wherever else her wanderlust takes her. But the creative journey truly blossoms in the studio attached to her house, where she transforms her finds into pillows with the help of a small band of women who cut out and restore the needlework and handle the sewing. For Christmas, leftover scraps are fashioned into mini stockings, perfect for hanging as ornaments, tying on packages, or holding little gifts. "They've become so popular that now I also look for fabrics specifically for them," the designer says.

Whenever Rebecca gets muddled working out a particular design, she wanders into the garden or through the nearby cotton fields and pecan orchard to clear her head and look for inspiration. "I call our area the Manhattan of flora and fauna," she says. "We may not have a lot of people, but we have a lot of plants." It doesn't take too long before the creative juices start flowing again, and thus the pillows do too, making their way into some of the most stylish interiors around the country.

When the couple determined to build their own house on a parcel of family property that overlooks Lake Bruin, Rebecca asked Michael Carbine, their architect, for something "part New Orleans, part lake house, part hunting lodge," she says. The house radiates a put-your-feet-up attitude mixed with a vibe of sophisticated eccentricity that comes from

Rebecca's love for European antiques, eclectic art painted by friends, and, of course, fine fabrics. "I love the look of old wood against concrete floors; a chandelier in the style of a crystal one, but made with wine corks instead; and the refinement of my pillows against white cotton slipcovers," she says. "If I had to put a name to my style, it would be 'patina.' I decorate with things that really have meaning for me—and warmth and spirit, like an old soul. Or maybe that's just a fancier way of saying a lot of our pieces already have a few dings and will survive our dog, Lucille."

Nature always plays an important role in the designer's narrative, certainly in the motifs she brings in through textiles, and also in the garden flowers and greenery, native to the property, that she uses to decorate indoors. "During the holidays, I cut as much as I can for decoration: magnolias to tuck in cupboards and garlands, sasanquas to float in bowls, and sometimes even roses, as it still can be 80 degrees in December and they'll be in bloom," she says. Outside, cedar boughs and ilex berries are threaded through ribbons hanging over the entrance, and even her dancing-bear topiary gets a little extra flair. He extends a joyful welcome to Locustland every day of the year, but never more than when he's carrying an armful of poinsettias and wearing a festive red bow tie. Even so, one can be sure he won't be the most dapper or colorful character in Rebecca and Michael's Christmas story.

RIGHT: The living room illustrates Rebecca's philosophy that the fine mixes happily with the casual. Lucille and Birdie Ann, a pair of Brittany Spaniels, lounge on a slipcovered sofa accented with the designer's velvet and Fortuny pillows. The wood-planked walls were originally painted a deeper red. FOLLOWING SPREAD, LEFT PAGE, CLOCKWISE FROM TOP LEFT: The entrance to Rebecca's house is festooned with ribbons, a garland, and topiaries. The house's red trim is played up with poinsettias and ribbon. Michael even dons red. Pillows with floral embroidery from Turkey, a headboard with eighteenth-century French embroidery, and a suzani coverlet from Uzbekistan make a guest bedroom particularly inviting. RIGHT PAGE: The decoration on a cake to be served after Christmas dinner mimics Rebecca's pillows.

REBECCA'S PICKS FOR LIVING FLORAL
ARRANGING AND DECORATING

We never know what Louisiana weather will be like in December. If we've had a hard frost, I'll rely on as much magnolia, cypress, and cedar as I can cut. If it's still warm, we'll have lots of camellias, which I put out in bowls.

I think about wrapping the same way I do pillow design: planning the color scheme, measuring, and adding in a little extra ornamentation. I love to use beautiful papers, such as a Florentine marble or a *faux bois*. If the box is large, I'll wrap the package in a solid color and layer the special paper over it. I'll tie on one of my fabric stockings or tuck in a sprig of greenery or a flower.

The pillows in my house come and go based on what sells, but at Christmastime, I make sure I have some in shades of red and green, although I prefer when the colors are less traditional, such as chartreuse and salmon. Pillows are one of the easiest ways to change the look of a room.

I love things that tell a story. We have a clay bust of my father-in-law that my husband, Michael, made in the seventh grade. We put hats on it throughout the year—a Fortuny one I've made or a New Orleans Saints cap during football season. Of course, at Christmastime he gets a Santa hat.

LIVING COLOR

Sybil Sylvester
Birmingham, Alabama

As a child, one of Sybil Sylvester's favorite pastimes was plopping down in the yard to pick wild violets for nosegays or daisies and dandelions to fashion into chains. On occasion her attention would wander over to neighboring gardens for more "cultivated" flowers. Many years later, that spark of free-spiritedness and her unfettered passion for flowers continue to enliven the arrangements and events she turns out from Wildflower Designs, her business of nearly thirty years. It thrives in the Birmingham, Alabama, home she shares with her husband, Bill. As she swings her front door open to welcome in friends for lunch, it almost feels as if she's inviting guests into one of her bouquets. Cheerful bursts of color beckon.

Floral motifs, as well as arrangements, nod hello from every room, and although it would seem obvious that someone in her profession would gravitate toward decor with a botanical bent, Sybil says she doesn't make those choices by design. "I'm simply guided by what I love. I take the elegant, knock it down a notch, and add in some nature," she says. "And I have to have something a bit funky or unusual to catch the eye. Otherwise things get too staid and calm for me." Thus, these are not classic English chintzes or demure wallflowers that decorate the Sylvesters' town house, but instead confident expressions and bold strokes. Her love of flowers may have begun with violets, but there are no shrinking ones to be had here.

Just as she connects certain flowers to memories, Sybil prefers her furnishings and art to have a strong personal pull. While she leans toward a more contemporary aesthetic, she softens the edges with family pieces and antiques. The bold, gold floral wallpaper in the elevator by friend and designer Ashley Woodson Bailey, mixed with a dainty gold antique bench and leopard rug,

is vintage Sybil. And the designer's black-and-white poppy wallpaper serves as a canvas for Sybil's approach to color blocking, as hot-pink and daffodil-yellow chairs hold their own against the graphic backdrop.

The decor may be eclectic, but then so is Sybil's floral-arranging sensibility. She eschews the idea of having one distinct style, preferring instead to take her cues from the occasion, the venue, and the personalities of her clients. "But I'll always be drawn to the loose and natural," she says. Early on, "I was going in my own yard and to my friends' and family's gardens to pick a little of this and a little of that to cobble together something pretty," she says. Today, her flower sources are pedigreed and plentiful. When she makes arrangements for her own home, she's still likely to snip a vine or branch from a nearby hillside or to pluck a blossom she spots along the road to drop into one of her favorite bud vases. Unlike fresh flowers, old habits, it appears, never die.

LEFT: Sybil Sylvester maintains that the container is as important as the arrangement. The floral designer found a series of colorful vases in A'Mano, a Birmingham shop, which stand on their own as art or can come alive when filled with greenery or branches. The painting by Dale Chihuly depicts the glass installation he designed for the Bellagio in Las Vegas. PREVIOUS SPREAD, RIGHT PAGE: The dining room is painted deep indigo to echo the wallpaper in the adjacent hallway. After Sybil posted a photograph on social media of a parade of dahlias on her table, artist Lila Graves asked if she could paint the scene. Months later, the painting was up for auction at a Birmingham antiques and garden show, and Sybil knew she had to have it.

SYBIL'S PICKS FOR LIVING FLORAL
ARRANGING

I use every part of the color wheel in my floral arrangements. Mother Nature has a vast range to choose from:

WARM TONES
Red: zinnia, butterfly ranunculus, long-stem gloriosa lily
Yellow: pincushion protea, *Mimosa floribunda,* tree peony
Orange: asclepias; sandersonia; 'Crown Imperial' fritillaria
Coral: godetia, ranunculus, 'Coral Charm' peony
Peach: poppy, quince, 'Juliet' rose
Pink: 'Blushing Bride' protea, nerine,
'Charlotte' Japanese bicolor ranunculus

COOL TONES
Green: 'Green Trick' dianthus, lotus pod, jasmine,
bells of Ireland, hellebore, viburnum
Blue: tweedia, hydrangea, forget-me-not
Purple: muscari, lilac, clematis
Aubergine: chocolate Queen Anne's lace,
anemone, *Fritillaria persica*

NEUTRAL TERRITORY
White: orlaya, nerine, lily of the valley
Cream: stock, 'Cheerfulness' narcissus, 'Yves Piaget' rose
Brown: scabiosa pods, chocolate sweet pea
Black: 'Blackberry Scoop' scabiosa, dahlia, 'Black Forest' calla lily

ABOVE: When Sybil and her husband moved to their town house, she hated to leave behind her garden. But they were so lucky to find a place with outdoor space. The couple frequently entertains on the porch, and Sybil creates an arrangement that looks as if it was gathered from the garden, with plants such as butterfly ranunculus, chocolate cosmos, and scabiosa sprouting from a copper vessel. OPPOSITE, CLOCKWISE FROM TOP LEFT: The elevator, a favorite spot of her spaniel, Gabby, is decorated with wallpaper by Ashley Woodson Bailey and an animal-print carpet. Whether in art or in the wild, Sybil is naturally drawn to all things floral. In the entry, a painting by Ben Johnson pops against Ashley Woodson Bailey's black-and-white wallpaper of poppies.

A LADIES LUNCHEON IN THE GROVE

Rebecca Gardner
Savannah, Georgia

Rebecca Gardner of Houses & Parties, an event and interiors specialist based in Savannah and New York, is someone who sings her own tune. She believes that rules are more like suggestions and that a little irreverence is in order. Her events always include a surprise. She's introduced a basket of bunnies for guests to play with at an outdoor wedding, decorated a table with withered leaves and flowers on the brink of decay, and served takeout Chinese straight out of the box on elegant Herend china. The novelty's never random, but rather is part of an orchestrated experience for those fortunate enough to attend a Rebecca event. She's like a child with a dress-up box who keeps reaching in and arranging things in completely new ways.

The location of an event drives many decisions when it comes to the mix of ingredients. When she held a baby shower at a former 1960s Getty filling station with an art installation of Lalanne sheep, she naturally chose a picnic theme with baskets brimming with gourmet fare and cut glass filled with Champagne. She imagined a dreamy ladies' luncheon in the middle of a camellia grove on an island just off of Savannah in February. She was inspired by the British photographer Tim Walker. "I wanted it to be a bit like going down Alice's rabbit hole, and plopping the table in the middle of the grove with no obvious path made getting to it a bit of an adventure in itself," she says. The timing was critical; she wanted the grove to be in full bloom and so was on "camellia watch" to get it just right. A bold pink-and-white-striped tablecloth, crisp white ruffled chair covers, ornate silver, and abundant cut camellias contributed to the decidedly feminine affair. The Champagne was pink as was the soup. She even included a few parlor games as icebreakers. "In today's busy world, going to a ladies' luncheon in the middle of the day is a luxury."

ABOVE: Rebecca Gardner's luncheon is a celebration of camellias. Many varieties of camellias dance in petite monogrammed glass vases from her collection on her table. OPPOSITE, CLOCKWISE FROM TOP LEFT: Rebecca, not above giving Mother Nature a little help, ties a few extra camellia stems to branches in preparation for the luncheon. Her table setting includes ornate repoussé silver, Herend Chinese Bouquet salad plates, mint julep cups from her personal collection, groupings of vibrant camellias in small glass vases, and lace-edged linen napkins on a lively pink-and-white striped tablecloth. The menu sits on a Mottahedeh plate in the Tobacco Leaf pattern. PREVIOUS SPREAD: The party was timed so the camellias would be in full bloom, creating a canopy over the table.

REBECCA'S PICKS FOR LIVING FLORAL

ENTERTAINING

Think about bringing something retro into the mix.
I decorate tables with piles of sugared fruit, which is so
outdated, it's funky.

Decor is important, but even more crucial is lighting.
Dim overhead lights and use candles at different heights.
Everyone feels beautiful in candlelight.

An obvious effort is always appreciated, and it
can come in many forms, from the food and decor to
the music and flowers. When guests see that effort,
they tend to behave accordingly.

Loose floral arrangements attract more interest than
uptight bunches. Let flowers spill onto the table.

Tablecloths can be fashioned from loose fabric, potted
plants can be centerpieces, and moss can be a table
runner. Look at using items that you have in fresh ways.

137

SOUTHERN CHARM WITH A GLOBAL VIEW

Barry Dixon
Warrenton, Virginia

Whether Barry Dixon decorates a penthouse in New York, a vacation getaway in the Caribbean, a palatial residence in Beijing, or an old Virginia farmhouse, his projects emanate an inherent instinctive sense of place, while speaking to intellectual curiosities and influences beyond the front door. Like an alchemist bent on turning lead into gold, the interior designer deftly blends and balances opposing elements—old with new, masculine with feminine, roughhewn with sleek, East with West—to concoct harmonious spaces that also exude an air of graciousness and ease, qualities Barry himself has in equal measure. When it comes to creating the kind of chemistry that makes you want to sit down in a room and never leave, Barry may well be the ultimate mix master.

Although he was born in Tennessee, Barry had a nomadic childhood. His father's career as a metals expert meant the family moved frequently to far-flung locales such as India, Korea, Pakistan, and South Africa as the elder Dixon pursued his research in metallurgy. Those early experiences shaped the designer's boundless enthusiasm for exploring and appreciating different cultures, but also, perhaps more surprisingly, gave him a strong sense of home. "My parents brought their Southern sensibility, warmth, and hospitality to each new place," says Barry. "The container of furniture would arrive, and the same dining chairs and sideboard would be unpacked. What went on or with them would change, but the familiarity of those pieces lent constancy."

Summers spent back in Tennessee with his grandmother, Nettie Darr, also kept Barry firmly in touch with his Southern roots. "Her philosophy, and now mine, was to make floral arrangements the way one should cook, always using the

freshest ingredients and what's in season. It's the way I grew up, with things very natural and unforced, and that's how I live and decorate."

After returning to the States for college at Ole Miss, Barry worked for designers in Washington, D.C., before opening his own Georgetown atelier. Then, in the late nineties, he finally found the place he wanted to permanently call home—Elway Hall, a stately 1907 Edwardian-style manor nestled amid three hundred acres in the horse country of Warrenton, Virginia. By day, his design staff buzzes with activity on the top floor. Meanwhile, Barry keeps on the move with decorating projects around the country and across the globe, numerous product design collaborations, and requests for speaking engagements.

Barry's sources of inspiration are far-reaching. A venture through a souk in Marrakesh inevitably leads to a trove of silver or antique textiles. The crystal-clear blue of the water in St. Barth's or the blazing oranges and reds of an African sunset reappear in schemes for upcoming projects. His imagination, however, can just as easily be kindled close to home, in a stroll down to the barn or on a trek through the woods to gather materials for an arrangement. Eggs from the Araucana hens or a border of dahlias in the cutting garden inspire the colors in his paint collection. The way a magnolia leaf curls up at its edges turns into a piece of furniture or lighting.

No matter where his work takes him, of one thing Barry is certain: nature will always be organic to his design process. "It's universally loved and celebrated in every culture, and I don't think I've ever decorated a house without some botanical reference," he says.

RIGHT: Barry loves the combination of rich apricot tones and pops of bright red in floral and ilex berry arrangements in this guest room at his Virginia house, Elway Hall. The japanned dressing table with swags of giltwood flowers provides a subtle floral reference. PREVIOUS PAGE: A living room evokes the ambience of an English gentlemen's club with oak-paneled walls, an antique pastoral oil painting, and a quartet of espresso-colored club chairs encircling a carved acanthus-based table. Edwardian-style flowers appliquéd to the chair backs illustrate that flowers are just as at home in spaces that have a masculine design sensibility. FOLLOWING SPREAD, LEFT PAGE, CLOCKWISE FROM TOP LEFT: Barry is never timid about using pattern: Honeysuckle & Tulip, an Arts and Crafts–era design by William Morris, covers the walls of his breakfast nook. He gathers ilex berries for decoration. The hounds and game found on a piece of brown-and-white transferware inspired Barry to create Warrenton Toile for Vervain. RIGHT PAGE: The designer loves to upholster dining room walls because it quiets the clatter of clinking glasses and silverware, so you can hear the conversation at the table. This dining room also includes more intimate seating for a cup of tea or after-dinner drink; the fabric is a tree-of-life print by Robert Kime.

BARRY'S PICKS FOR LIVING FLORAL
DECORATING

I incorporate many different floral patterns in the same room, finding some way to connect one to the other via color and scale, almost like arranging complementary flowers in a vase.

When a room has awkward architecture, such as an attic bedroom, I'll wallpaper both the walls and ceiling with a floral pattern to make the odd angles disappear.

I'm always fascinated by trees, and I re-create their effect indoors by using branches in a towering arrangement to create interesting shadows from light overhead.

My color palette will often draw from the vistas through the windows, so we can recall their grace and power after the sun sets.

I use indigenous species of flora and fauna to tether a home to its location. For example, tendrils of fern, tree leaves and branches, or even a deer or two might appear in a fabric pattern or a mural for a mountain retreat.

A guest bedroom with walls or the drapery blooming with bright bouquets of colorful flowers is a cheerful way to welcome guests into your home. A fragrant bedside arrangement—the simpler the better—is the icing on the cake.

ABOVE: A series of botanicals by Washington, D.C., artist John Matthew Moore are hung close together, creating the effect of flowers blooming through windowpanes. OPPOSITE: Hand-painted wallpaper by Gracie gives guests the feeling that they are dining in a garden conservatory. A silver punch bowl holds flowers in shades of spring green.

SPRING

DINING IN THE MEADOW

P. Allen Smith
Moss Mountain Farm, Arkansas

"While I love the quiet and tranquility of the farm, I equally love when Moss Mountain is animated with people enjoying it. That's when the spaces really come to life," says landscape and garden designer P. Allen Smith about his five-hundred-acre Arkansas farm. The popularity of the place came as a surprise to Allen, who initially conceived Moss Mountain as a private estate when he purchased the property in 2004. He reconsidered his stance and began plans to shift the farm to a more public-friendly venue when fans of his seventeen-season PBS series *P. Allen Smith's Garden Home* began contacting him, wanting to come visit and tour the farm.

"Interest grew as folks watched my show and saw the farm's development unfold," Allen says. "I started getting letters from them wanting to see the place for themselves." The more he thought about it, the more he realized that these requests mirrored his own desire to share his knowledge of sustainable living and hands-on gardening with others. Since 2009, when the public was first invited to explore the grounds, Allen has led countless groups through the farm's apple-orchard allées and up Daffodil Hill, which fully lives up to its name each spring.

The one-acre vegetable garden at Moss Mountain is home to raised beds filled with organic edible and ornamental produce and flowers. "I rely on the garden for every event where there's a meal prepared, but it's also important that I keep an eye on how much of the garden stays put. The same can be said about the flowers, foliage, and grasses used in arrangements and table settings on the farm."

Besides his passion for growing things, Allen is well versed in the history of garden design, having devoted his graduate studies to English gardens while at the University of Manchester in England. In particular, he was drawn to the British estate grounds visited by John Adams and Thomas Jefferson in the eighteenth century, along with the concurrent landscape design movement known as *ferme ornée,* or ornamental farm. "It was this concept of *ferme ornée* that influenced my layout of Moss Mountain, in which the farm is both functional and arranged in outdoor 'rooms' that display a mix of annuals, herbs, perennials, roses, shrubs, and ornamental grasses," Allen says.

The farm's crowning centerpiece, a 350-year-old oak tree named Big Sister Oak, presides over the property, which includes sweeping views of the Arkansas River. "Big Sister Oak is my North Star. Even the house is sited in line with it," he says.

Allen's affinity for historic landscapes is coupled with his admiration for the Greek Revival period, which inspired his home's design and many of the outbuildings at Moss

RIGHT: The shade of the branches of Big Sister Oak is a popular spot for alfresco dining. P. Allen Smith's horse, Trudy, grazes in the background. PREVIOUS PAGE: Allen chose a circular layout for the "room" of the terrace garden, which overlooks the Arkansas River. The vase-shaped chaste tree (of the *Vitex* genus) bestows a regal note.

Mountain. "I modeled the main house after an 1840s Greek Revival farmhouse but gave it a twist by building it in an eco-friendly manner with sustainable materials," he says. "Since the farm as a collective property dates back to that period, both structures and land maintain a direct link to that era."

In order to instill an extra note of authenticity, Allen designed two mirror dependencies behind the main residence that accommodate a summer kitchen and an artist's studio. Even the large chicken house where Allen keeps his heritage poultry exhibits similar styling. Considering all the efforts and influences that continue to enrich this well-tended place, it seems only natural now that Allen's devotees, along with the curious and the weekend gardeners, can experience it as well, learning a thing or two along the way.

ABOVE: The terrace garden features broad, grassy walking paths. OPPOSITE, CLOCKWISE FROM TOP LEFT: An alfresco gathering allows Allen to show off his green thumb as well as his hospitality. A bouquet incorporates flowers grown at Moss Mountain Farm, including 'Pink Impression' tulips, 'Coral Sunset' peonies, 'Sonnet' snapdragons, and 'Orange Wonder' freesia. When Allen sets the table, he likes to use items from his collections, like the bird bud vases, which hold stems of 'Orange Wonder' freesia and German chamomile. A leaf with gold lettering serves as a place card, set in one of the designer's many vintage flower frogs.

ALLEN'S PICKS FOR LIVING FLORAL
ENTERTAINING

At Moss Mountain Farm, the first thing we do is hand visitors a drink. Without fail, that gesture sets a tour on the right track.

I always create flower and foliage arrangements based on what's in bloom in the gardens. Such efforts further connect the farm's events with the beauty of the outdoors—particularly when the event is held indoors.

Special mementos such as my bird bud vases, which I use for spring brunches, add a personal layer to the table.

153

A TASTE FOR FLOWERS

Suzanne Rheinstein
Los Angeles, California

Despite years of living in Los Angeles, California, decorator Suzanne Rheinstein possesses a razor-sharp Southern sensibility. She developed it during a childhood spent basking in the romantic influence of New Orleans, her hometown, and honed it as an adult exploring the wide world of timelessly beautiful houses and gardens. Now she spreads the easy traditionalism of Southern style through the houses she designs for clients around the world and through her books, *Rooms for Living* and *At Home*.

Suzanne's New Orleans childhood was an immersive experience in classic style. "When I was a child, my mother took courses all over the South in gardening, which was very unusual for her time," she says. "My grandmother was also a wonderful gardener and my next-door neighbor was Gerrie Bremermann, a doyenne of New Orleans decorating. I had all these women around me who loved doing things for their houses and their gardens."

In her work for clients and in her own homes, Suzanne conjures an enticing point of view, blurring boundaries between outside and in, and channeling design influences as wide-ranging as gardens in the South of France and English country houses. "Part of my garden was inspired by Nicole de Vésian, the head of design at Hermès for many years, who had an extraordinary garden in Provence that I was so fortunate to visit," she recalls. "She used a lot of gravel in her gardens, which was also a perfect solution to gardening in our Southern California climate."

Her own garden evolved over time and reflects her openness to influence. "When my husband, Fred, and I moved into our house in Hancock Park, we budgeted for the garden," she says. "I was so ambitious, however, that I spent the entire amount on the front of the house. I wanted a stilt hedge—like

SUZANNE'S PICKS FOR LIVING FLORAL
ARRANGING AND DECORATING

My favorite flowers to send are seasonal—masses of sweet peas in the spring; dahlias, especially the shaggy café au lait ones, in the summer; rose hips or orange or red berries in the fall and around the holidays; and white amaryllis in a tall cylinder in the winter.

For a quick and simple centerpiece, I use my collections of small containers, which I fill with bits and pieces from the garden. If it's super casual, I'll put berries, herbs, and kumquats in quirky lead pieces. When entertaining in my dining room, I'll cluster flowers in toning colors, like all shades of pink, in various old etched-glass vessels.

The quickest way to bring the outside in is to whack off part of a bush or tree in the garden and bring it inside. In the fall, I'll buy reddish-brown oak leaves from the florist to have my own romantic tree gracing the living room.

My favorite floral fabrics include Colefax and Fowler's Bailey Rose in the chartreuse and purply-brown colorway and a Brunschwig & Fils linen print called Walpole in the cabbage-rose colorway. It's on French slipper chairs in my New York bedroom and I never tire of it. I worked on a linen print with Lee Jofa called Garden Roses, and my entire living room has slipcovers of Garden Roses in slate and beige.

ABOVE: Suzanne Rheinstein's parterre garden, known as the secret garden, is graphic yet lush, and provides a variety of options for bringing the outside in. OPPOSITE, CLOCKWISE FROM TOP LEFT: Fresh purple clematis in a nineteenth-century French tole tiered container, French and English floral watercolors, and an Italian painted chest with clusters of blooms on the drawers speak to the designer's love of art, antiques, and flowers. Suzanne, an avid gardener, loves to cut greenery and blooms from her California parterre garden for arrangements inside. A silver heirloom julep cup with casually arranged roses gathered from the garden is ideal for a powder room. PREVIOUS PAGE: In a bedroom, Suzanne brought in flowers without visiting the florist through wallpaper that depicts porcelain vases perched in blossoming branches that climb the walls above the fireplace and a bird's nest spilling robin's eggs onto the mantel. Chinoiserie lamps on lacquered side tables add a deft touch of black.

LEFT: Lifelike porcelain-and-tole pieces by Ukrainian-born sculptor Vladimir Kanevsky add another layer of flowers to Suzanne's interior designs. OPPOSITE: Details make the difference in Suzanne's work. In a girl's bedroom, she paired a hand-screened print from Raoul Textiles on the upholstery with a skinny-striped cotton fabric on the walls. Raspberry trim on the bed and a matching canopy lining add decorator polish.

the kind I had seen in some of the grand European gardens we had visited—in the worst kind of way. I ripped out all the hybrid tea roses, which of course irritated the grande dames of the neighborhood. All I can say is thank goodness I didn't have all the resources to do everything I wanted to do."

Suzanne's interior design radiates a fresh interpretation of traditional style. Florals are nothing new to homes since the 1940s, when Colefax and Fowler bedecked London living rooms in floral prints that came to epitomize aristocratic British style. But in Suzanne's hands, they become new again, rendered in current color preferences and mixed with stripes or checks. "Floral fabrics are coming back in a big way, but you still have to be careful," she says. "I know that some people are still frightened when they hear the word 'chintz,' but it can feel totally fresh and fabulous."

When she entertains, which she does frequently and with the ease of a Southerner, Suzanne serves delicious food and sets a glorious table, always with a floral centerpiece. "I cut flowers from the garden for my arrangements. I'll use different flowers in the same color and put them in similar kinds of containers, then scatter them all around the dining table," she says. "I try to live by a quote of Joan Didion's I once read about why she uses her good silver every day: 'Every day is all there is.'"

LOWCOUNTRY LUXE

Calder Clark
Charleston, South Carolina

Calder Clark's professional life is always a party. Known as one of the nation's premier wedding and event designers, she plans dreamy weddings and VIP functions, overseeing every aspect from the grandest gesture down to the smallest boutonnière. One might think that that would kick the pressure—and expectations—up a notch or two when she hosts a party of her own. Calder dismisses the notion with a wave of her hand. "Entertaining is in my blood. I grew up in a family that loved to spoil others with hospitality and good food, and I enjoy carrying on those traditions."

Calder honed her event-planning and catering skills with renowned firm Design Cuisine in Washington, D.C., where she oversaw such marquee affairs as George W. Bush's inaugural luncheon, as well as weddings for A-list names like Carnegie and Rockefeller. Eventually love and the Lowcountry beckoned her to Charleston, and after a few years of orchestrating functions for a local hotel, she opened her own business. Now she takes on a limited number of highly customized events, infusing each one with an eye for detail, the element of surprise, and a bit of whimsy mixed in with some drop-dead glamour.

Although Calder choreographs chic receptions for hundreds without batting an eyelash, she and her husband, Chauncey, prefer more relaxed parties at home, usually of no more than eight. But that hardly means that Calder's party-planning prowess takes the day off. "I want guests to feel as though we've set a beautiful table just for them, but never to feel stiff themselves. My style is inherently casual with the occasional elegant swish."

160

LEFT: Whether it's large or small, event designer Calder Clark wants a party to have polish without seeming overwrought. Having a bar cart set up in her courtyard allows guests to help themselves while she attends to last-minute details. PREVIOUS PAGE AND OPPOSITE, TOP LEFT: Calder sets the table in icy tones of white and blue, including a lush centerpiece of tulips. Fresh juices and garnishes, such as pomegranate seeds and lemon curls, are meant to be mixed with Champagne or sparkling water, and they introduce a touch of bright color. OPPOSITE, TOP RIGHT AND BOTTOM LEFT: Calder describes her personal style as "inherently casual with the occasional elegant swish." Here she balances the cool palette with warm metallics, including gold bamboo flatware. Raw oysters are served from a vintage Danish bathtub. TOP LEFT: Gold-rimmed and etched crystal mix with colored glass, illustrating Calder's preference for keeping things from being too "matchy-matchy."

She prefers setting the stage in her courtyard, especially in the early spring, when Charleston's temperate clime frequently obliges. "That's a time of year when people long to be outdoors. Dining feels a bit like an unexpected picnic," says Calder. However, there'll be no pesky ants, paper plates, or sitting on the ground at this affair. She believes in bringing the inside out, and that means pretty throws and velvet pillows tucked in wicker chairs, and pulling from her considerable stash of china, crystal, flatware, and linens for the weathered teak table. Nothing is too precious to be considered.

Calder establishes the mood with a palette of smoky grays and blues, and a springy white tulip centerpiece with silvery lamb's ears. Champagne and oysters will be the stars on the menu, but to keep things from getting too fancy, she injects a dash of playfulness with a vintage Danish bathtub used to serve the oysters.

Dessert will be served by the outdoor fireplace. "I like to keep things cozy, both literally and figuratively," says Clark, "with a cashmere blanket for the early spring coastal breeze, ever-flowing bubbly, and s'mores by the fire."

CALDER'S PICKS FOR LIVING FLORAL
ENTERTAINING AND ARRANGING

Just because you can, doesn't mean you should. Every course doesn't have to be homemade; all the tableware doesn't have to be the finest of the fine, or polished to a gleam. It's okay to cobble it together a little and to be real.

Sometimes I'm a "dessert before dinner" kind of girl. Rules are made to be broken. Champagne glasses can hold water; red wine can be served in water goblets. Antique silver and gold electroplate flatware mix beautifully on the table. The only rule I'll never break is avoiding the use of floral centerpieces that block conversation.

Things on the table should be kissing cousins, as opposed to obsessively coordinated. No one wants to be "bride in a bag," where everything matches perfectly.

"The ornament of a house is the friends who frequent it." Ralph Waldo Emerson said this first, but I translate it to not fussing too much over everything, particularly after the guests have arrived. People matter most. Be present and untethered, and just drink in the conversation—and the wine.

Calder gravitates toward a floral-arranging style that is "not too loose, not too composed, but something in between," she says. "A monochromatic and mono-botanical composition always works, particularly if you're not an experienced floral designer. She loves flowers with "pretty faces," such as lush double tulips.

165

NATURAL HISTORY

Thomas Jayne
New York, New York

Growing up in Southern California, interior designer Thomas Jayne exhibited a natural curiosity about history, particularly when it came to his family's garden. "We had plants that belonged to our forebears, and I loved hearing stories that the Dalbergia was once on Aunt Molly's front porch, or that a Strelitzia came from a cutting introduced to San Diego in 1890," says Thomas. "I was intrigued that we could have a flower that was identical to one my great-grandmother grew, so that in a sense we were sharing something beautiful across time."

Appreciating that kind of organic connection between past and present might have seemed rather a precocious notion for a child, but it's one that has only continued to flourish throughout Thomas's life and career. He obtained a degree in architecture and a master's in American material culture and decorative arts, with an eye toward becoming a curator. Soon after he was offered an assistant's position at the venerable New York design firm Parish-Hadley, and then spent time working for another design icon, Kevin McNamara. His work experience helped cultivate his decorating skills before he opened his own Manhattan studio nearly thirty years ago.

True to his academic training, Thomas's interiors speak of his love of classic architecture and details, respect for tradition, and reverence for exquisite craftsmanship. "It's hard to have a fine room with bad architecture, but one with classical proportions can get enriched to any level, whether the furnishings are contemporary or antique," says Thomas. "I am reminded of my mother's maxim, 'Don't put flower arrangements in a dirty house.' You have to have the house in order before you decorate."

Although he has become known for incorporating antiques and fine art that often come with impeccable pedigrees, the designer's work feels

anything but beholden to the past or museum-like. The spaces he creates are intended to be stylish reflections of the lives that are being lived in them, thus it's very much the client's present narrative that matters most.

Nature often plays a strong character in the stories Thomas tells through decoration, whether it's maximizing the relationship of a house to its garden, considering the way environmental light impacts his palette decisions, or choosing the botanical motifs he uses throughout. "When I think about it, so many of my clients are also great gardeners. People who grow things tend to be pretty sophisticated thinkers," says Thomas. "The outside world presents us with things we might not have dreamed of otherwise—shapes, forms, and color combinations. I'll do a scheme and then realize we need a printed floral linen or something organic to make it all work. Nature and flowers are bridges—they transcend all design elements, styles, and class boundaries."

RIGHT: Thomas Jayne believes the outside is as important as what's inside when decorating, but when a room doesn't have an interesting view, he'll create one. In this bedroom, he used a scenic wallpaper by Gracie. "There's always a lush landscape for the owner to wake up to," he says. PREVIOUS PAGE: When Thomas decorated this apartment, the art was to come later. One such piece turned out to be a Picasso. "It's a misconception that fine paintings have to be displayed on white walls," he says. "Green is nature's neutral. It works with anything." FOLLOWING SPREAD, LEFT PAGE, CLOCKWISE FROM TOP LEFT: "When you're working in a traditional design vernacular, it's easier not to go out of style. Quality always endures," says Thomas. "It might not be the latest trend, but it will still look good." The New York–based designer uses floral fabrics, but in a restrained way, as he did in a New Orleans parlor with club chairs upholstered in chintz by Le Manach. The designer, who grew up in a family of gardeners, carries on the tradition in his own way. He planted more than three hundred daffodil bulbs in a public median near his New York apartment. A few have made their way into his home. In a neoclassical country house that Thomas designed, the yellow master bedroom features a bed reputed to have belonged to Duncan Phyfe's sister. It is trimmed in a subtle tone-on-tone floral pattern on the valance, and the yellow theme is picked up in an explosion of daffodils. RIGHT PAGE: Thomas maintains a second home in New Orleans, where he painted the sitting room a Creole pink. A toile de Jouy by Schumacher carries through the French thread, and deep-pink camellias in a silver Jefferson cup on a side table provide a fresh, Southern accent.

THOMAS'S PICKS FOR LIVING FLORAL
ARRANGING, GARDENING, AND DECORATING

I love camellias as well as underdog flowers such as gladiolas, even though I know they're not chic. They're very 1930s and old-fashioned.

Constance Spry is my favorite floral designer. Her book *Party Flowers* shows pictures of arrangements she did for the 1953 coronation of Queen Elizabeth II, with red flowers from every country in the commonwealth displayed with gold lamé.

I prefer simple floral containers with texture. I collect early 1920s matte green florist vases. They're real workhorses, and look good in almost any interior.

Russell Page, Frederick Law Olmsted, and Capability Brown were masters of landscape design. Olmsted's ability to take natural elements and render them appropriately for an urban setting and how he anticipated how things were going to look in one hundred years are lessons I try to apply in my own work.

Chintz sometimes gets maligned. I like to use it more like Colefax and Fowler would have, in a tailored, restrained way. I'll pair a chintz chair with a natural rug or with muslin curtains rather than silk taffeta. If you put classic patterns such as Lee Jofa's Althea or Colefax and Fowler's Hydrangea with unexpected materials like leather or burlap, they'll look fresh.

COTTAGE LIVING

Frances Schultz
East Hampton, New York

A decade ago, when Frances Schultz and her then fiancé bought the charming but dilapidated Bee Cottage in East Hampton, New York, she never imagined the house would lead her through a journey of personal discovery. The invitations were already sent and received when Frances canceled her wedding. "Good man, bad match," she explains succinctly. Unsure of her next steps, Frances turned her attention to the needy house with the added intention of chronicling its recovery in the pages of *House Beautiful* magazine. But then, as she says, "A funny thing happened along the way. Unwittingly at first and then unavoidably, renovating the house became a metaphor for renovating myself."

She expanded on the *House Beautiful* columns in her book *The Bee Cottage Story: How I Made a Muddle of Things and Decorated My Way Back to Happiness.* "It was my haven, my spirit home. It healed me, and the outdoors was as much a part of that balm as the interiors," she wrote. Frances was able to create a house and garden that celebrated her life. The process also allowed her to indulge her passion for color—with a palette of white and green, blue and gray, brown and turquoise, and a dash of red, "because every house needs a dash of red." Her jewel-like garden in the back of Bee Cottage reflects the same playful use of color, with beds of pink lilies and roses, purple delphiniums, red bee balm, breezy white cosmoses, and dinner plate–size dahlias in every shade of pink and white imaginable, with a border of lush boxwood that ribbons around the pool and green space.

"The house filled up with ad hoc collections of art, rocks, shells, bird's nests, my mother's Staffordshire, my travel mementos, and more china

than is legal without a permit—quietly exuberant with pretty slipcovers and lovely linens because every house needs those too." Her efforts resulted in a house and garden that joyfully express her singular point of view. Her signature space, though, would have to be the garden room. With its green-and-white scheme, lattice wallpaper, and floral fabric, it is a bridge to the lush outside just beyond.

Throughout her rooms, Frances favors flowers with a looser, more natural feel. "I like pretty,

lush arrangements with flowers from my garden, but also with a bit of random, scavenged woodsy greenery woven in," she says. "Flowers that look intentional but not 'done.'"

With the rescue of Bee Cottage standing as a testament to her resilience, vision, and taste, that floral philosophy resounds through every aspect of her life. Though Frances moved to California and sold the house to a friend, it lives on in her writing and in her soul.

ABOVE: The patio of Bee Cottage is the most lived-in space of the house between April and November. A removable canvas cover shades the pergola. OPPOSITE: A bold-print tablecloth brings festivity to a café table and chairs beneath the vine-covered pergola. PREVIOUS PAGE: Frances wallpapered the garden room's walls in a trellis pattern by Carlton V. The sofa fabric is by Manuel Canovas. The chairs are from Katharine Hepburn's estate. FOLLOWING SPREAD, LEFT PAGE, CLOCKWISE FROM TOP LEFT: Hydrangeas and dahlias from the garden make an easy centerpiece. Blue-and-white plates and an oversize metal chalkboard dress up the back corner of the galley kitchen, where Frances often created flower arrangements. Shallow shelves were built in the stair hall to house a portion of Frances's collection of Staffordshire figurines. RIGHT PAGE: Pink dahlias and hydrangeas complement the living room's palette. "The flowers are a room's corsage—the simpler, the chicer," says Frances.

FRANCES'S PICKS FOR LIVING FLORAL
ENTERTAINING AND ARRANGING

I map everything in advance and tick off items throughout the week ahead, from the bar setup to which serving platters I'll use to what I'm wearing. All these little decisions take time, and eliminating them enables you to focus on your guests from the moment they arrive.

I much prefer to entertain in the open air, starting with drinks on the loggia and moving to dinner in the garden. But if it's oppressively hot, buggy, or humid, I have no problem shifting gears and setting the table indoors.

I'm lucky to have good flower sources, whether from my own garden or from local markets. But in a pinch, I'm not above grocery-store bouquets or roadside cuttings, especially since I lean toward loose bunches of mixed blooms in low containers for conversational convenience, or a mass of small mismatched vessels, each holding just a bloom or two. It's a small effort that creates a big impact. Whatever you do, do plenty of it. Nothing is worse than looking skimpy.

the bee cottage story

STYLISH SHEDS AND ELEGANT HIDEAWAYS PRINZING

THE INTIMATE GARDEN GORDON HAYWARD & MARY HAYWARD

THE ART ELEGANCE MARSHALL WATSON

FARM TO TABLE

Christopher Spitzmiller
Millbrook, New York

I t's always inspiring to know someone who has not only pursued their passion but also persevered through a season of challenge and failure to attain brilliant success. Christopher Spitzmiller is such a person. Born and bred in Buffalo, New York, he evinced an interest in pottery in prep school, and spent every free minute at the wheel and kiln. He developed into a proficient ceramicist and was offered the coveted artist-in-residence position at Southampton, New York's tony emporium, Mecox Gardens. It was there that he almost threw in the proverbial towel. He confesses, "Every pot I threw that summer cracked and broke. I thought it was a sign, but I just couldn't give it up."

Fast-forward a few years to when Christopher received a commission for two double-gourd vases from designer/friend Richard Keith Langham, who transformed the vases into table lamps for a client, and the brand was born. Influenced by classical forms and his love of good design, Christopher committed to creating and marketing lustrous works of art that just happen to be table lamps, to which he later added cachepots and tableware.

At his historic country home, Clove Brook Farm in Millbrook, New York, Christopher takes the same meticulous care with his decorating, gardening, and entertaining as he does with his ceramics. He's even installed a studio in one of the outbuildings so that he's never too far from his creations. With the soul of an artist and armed with the experience of a stint planning events in the Clinton White House, Christopher's farm gatherings are marvelous to behold. Before dinner, guests get a tour of the farm. His tables are gorgeous and inviting. He cuts from his copious lilac bushes in the spring and roses and dahlias in the summer, and arranges them in any one of his various signature cachepots. He also harvests fresh vegetables from the garden for delicious homemade dishes, which might be served on his own thrown dinnerware.

CHRISTOPHER'S PICKS FOR LIVING FLORAL
ARRANGING AND DECORATING

I keep my lilacs fresher longer by pounding the stems and recutting them at a forty-five-degree angle so that they can drink more easily.

Many prefer low table flowers, and I understand that, but I like more volume and height for impact. If that impedes conversation, I'm not above moving the flowers to a windowsill or side table—after the initial reveal, of course. They're still present and visible that way.

We've been growing grape hyacinths on the farm and I think they're perfect for bud vases, in the powder room, or added to each place setting. They blend beautifully with all the purple lilacs I inevitably use in the spring for my centerpieces.

Bring a garden indoors with a botanical painted wallpaper. When decorating my table, I like to pull colors from the paper, which makes everything flow visually.

ABOVE: Christopher Spitzmiller's matte-white *faux bois* cachepots are filled with lilacs, roses, and peonies and echo the white of the Frances Elkins loop chairs and china. OPPOSITE, CLOCKWISE FROM TOP LEFT: Christopher uses his own floral-patterned dinnerware, mixing it in with antique iconic Dodie Thayer lettuce ware. The host adds a finishing touch of purple wild hyacinths in bud vases at each setting. A modern take on a sunburst sconce in a rose-colored metal contrasts with the antique Chinese painted paper. PREVIOUS PAGE: The gate leading into Clove Brook Farm, Christopher's country retreat.

ROOMS FOR FLOWERS

Alex Papachristidis
New York, New York

For almost thirty years, designer Alex Papachristidis has been infusing houses with a fresh and elegant perspective. While there is a decidedly old-school quality to both his decorating style and his manners, his rooms—and his love of social media—are anything but old-fashioned. The born-and-bred New Yorker fashions rooms known for their bold use of color, pattern, books, and flowers, perfectly suited to the uptown clientele he serves. But his work is anything but stuffy. "Beauty is important because it nourishes the soul," he says. "But I don't think a beautiful room has to be uncomfortable. Upholstery and curtains create softness and luxury, while wood floors, sisal, and carpets add warmth and coziness. I believe in lots of lamps and lampshades—they add a certain kind of romance. And arrangements of flowers are like the icing on the cake. Their beauty makes a room sing. Rooms should be flattering and make people feel—and look—good."

Although all of his projects reflect his traditional sensibility, there's no uniformity in his work. "I try to make each project personal," he says. "I love to bring artisans into a home to make it look unique. And I try never to use a statement printed fabric more than once. Homes should have touches that reflect the homeowner's interests, so I encourage clients to find something they enjoy collecting." Nonetheless, there are certain principles he deploys consistently. Floral prints appear frequently in his work, like the tree-of-life print in which he swathed a client's dressing room—walls, daybed, and canopy. "There's something so comfortable about a floral chintz, which has the beauty of flowers that live forever in a room."

182

LEFT: Floral prints appear often in Alex Papachristidis's work, here in a Gracie wall covering with hand-painted peonies and apple blossoms that envelops the foyer. OPPOSITE: Alex masterfully mixes modern with ornate in a dining room with an Alexander Liberman painting, Jansen chandelier, and Brunschwig & Fils floral-patterned tapestry. A luscious mix of fruits and flowers crowns the table. PREVIOUS PAGE: A dressing room designed by Alex showcases his inherent love of vibrant patterns, luxurious fabric treatments, pretty lampshades, and animal prints.

"Fabrics set the whole backdrop for a room," he says, "and they give the first impression. When working with fabrics, it's about a variety of textures and scale—a big print and a small print with a woven, with a velvet, with a wool. I am drawn to Fortuny fabrics because they have a sense of history, and also because every dye lot is different, so each fabric feels custom. I also like incorporating tribal and ethnic elements because our eyes relate to them as cultural and historic. And I almost always use Le Manach's tiger- or leopard-print silk velvet as an accent. Animal prints bring strength and presence to a room, but I use them as neutrals."

In contrast to his old-school style, Alex is also a master of modern technology. His popular Instagram account serves as a diary of his impressions, featuring his home, his travels, and his Yorkshire terrier, Teddy. "Instagram has really changed my eye—I look at everything in a photographic way that I didn't before."

Alex Papachristidis chose a medley of horticulturally themed elements for his bedroom: a tree-patterned Swedish wallpaper from Old World Weavers along with a flowery batik spread, a Fortuny botanical print on a bergère chair, and even a trellis-patterned carpet by Beauvais, named for his beloved mother, Mariya. The tiny chair upholstered in leopard print provides the designer's dog, Teddy, easy access to the bed.

ALEX'S PICKS FOR LIVING FLORAL

DECORATING AND ENTERTAINING

Your home should always be ready for a party. I don't ever want to have to say, "Don't come over. My place is a mess."

Always be prepared by having bottles of Champagne, Perrier, and Coca-Cola on hand, as well as olives, delicious cheeses, and gourmet potato chips.

My favorite gift is cut flowers. Practically nothing makes me happier or brings me more joy—especially if they're from Zezé or Plaza Flowers in Manhattan.

Even if you haven't grown, received, or ordered fresh flowers, plant-filled patterns can provide a sense of the beauty of flowers that lives forever.

Above all, just forget about worrying that things will get damaged. You can have fifty people over and nothing gets broken, but it only takes one person with a Frappuccino—which you can be certain will spill over everything.

ABOVE: A bold, graphic black-and-white floral painting by Christopher Wool adds a modern moment to a crisp, classical dining room. The Regency table is suitably graced with a silver-footed urn full of white peonies and roses. OPPOSITE, CLOCKWISE FROM TOP LEFT: A small, lush arrangement of viburnums, deep purple hydrangeas, lisianthuses, and eryngiums completes Alex's richly appointed desk set. The designer poses with his Yorkshire terrier, Teddy. Never one to shy away from pattern, Alex combined six fabrics on his sofa and added another on the lampshades—floral arrangements always complement his mix of patterns.

189

A Cowtan & Tout floral wall covering and a pair of wicker daybeds sporting Clarence House floral linen cushions make for a cozy and inviting sunroom in Alex's family's country home. An elegant and sculptural white phalaenopsis orchid tucked into the corner provides a subtle, natural accent.

A WELL-PLANNED BRUNCH

Tara Guérard
Charleston, South Carolina

Event designer Tara Guérard seemed to burst onto the Charleston style scene in the late nineties, with her completely fresh way of imagining elegant parties. But, of course, her journey began long before that when, as a child, she saved her allowance to redecorate her room repeatedly, always enchanted by a new look. During college years, she worked at restaurants to fund her degree. Later, as head of a food–industry staffing service, she immersed herself in the elements of hospitality, from delicious food to the attention to ambience, and discovered her true calling.

Initially, Tara wanted a no-wedding business, focusing instead on more intimate (and less fraught) celebrations. But after her work began garnering the attention of magazines, demand from betrothed clients wore down her resistance. Now she's bringing her attention to detail to about eight weddings a year in locations all over the United States and Europe. A crew of up to one hundred off-duty firemen builds the elaborate sets she envisions, creating "transportive" events complete with rugs, furniture, fabrics, flowers, and food.

For smaller events, Tara brings the same exacting attention to detail she lavishes on weddings. When she threw a brunch for visiting fashion designer Lela Rose, who was in Charleston for Wedding Week, all her party tricks were on display. Paper goods are always a priority, so much so that in 2006, she launched a paper company, the Lettered Olive. Lela happens to share her enthusiasm. "She likes a handwritten invitation," says Tara, "so we started there." Because Lela's book, *Prêt-à-Party,* had just been published, she

TARA'S PICKS FOR LIVING FLORAL

ARRANGING, GARDENING, AND DECORATING

I always have a blooming orchid in the house, but anything that is blooming outside, I bring indoors—such as camellias in the winter and azaleas in the early spring. I'm constantly filling little vases for the guest bathroom or bringing in pretty leaves and branches for the urn by the fireplace.

The things I love best in my garden are fig vines, mandevilla vines, flowering dogwoods, magnolia trees, hydrangeas, crepe myrtles, forsythias, climbing roses, camellias, azaleas, geraniums, herbs, giant elephant's ears, Carolina jasmines, impatiens, cassias, and alliums. Any or all of these are most likely going to find their way into vases in my house before their bloom is over.

I like floral patterns and textures, especially embroidered pieces. I make tablecloths with floral motifs that have a tailored fit with inverted pleats.

Peonies are a favorite, but I'm obsessed with the double pearl tuberose that blooms in my garden.

I prefer smallish, looser, and more casual arrangements of flowers, but when a bigger, formal design is called for, I recommend a medium-size vintage footed urn with a big frog already inside: ready, set—arrange.

ABOVE: For a brunch celebrating Lela Rose's book, *Prêt-à-Party,* Tara Guérard set up a Bloody Mary bar equipped with fresh juices, pickled garnishes, and mixers. An armload of pink roses and peonies spiked with orange kumquats towered over the offerings. The juice blends wore snappy labels by the Lettered Olive. An array of garnishes allowed guests to customize their cocktails. OPPOSITE, CLOCKWISE FROM TOP LEFT: A coral cruiser bedecked with balloons greeted guests arriving at the brunch. A signed copy of Lela's book was the perfect party favor. Tara preps pink peonies for one of her arrangements. A tiered acrylic stand that she found at an antiques mall presents a variety of biscuits. PREVIOUS SPREAD: A loose bouquet of pink blossoms extends the cheerful party palette to a low table.

delighted even the guest of honor with a surprise book signing.

"Lela also likes a good drink, so we ran with that and created a Bloody Mary bar," says Tara. Along with two varieties of mixers and liquors, she also presented a colorful array of garnishes, including very Southern pickled okra and the always tasty celery. Guests could also choose from fresh juices, including a red blend of apple, beet, carrot, and ginger, and a green juice of kale, spinach, parsley, romaine, celery, cucumber, apple, lemon, and ginger. Pretty, calligraphed labels identified the

offerings. Biscuits served on a tiered stand included three types: Callie's Charleston biscuits, Anne's cheese biscuits, and ham biscuits, a standard at every Southern brunch.

The pairing of pink and coral is a signature of Tara Guérard Soirée and brings its festive mood to her brunch. Pink peonies and roses and kumquat branches spill from containers on the bar and on low tables. A bunch of balloons, tied to the handlebars of a Soirée bicycle, bobbed in the breeze at the front door, suggesting that revelry had arrived at Tara's home.

LOVE OF COUNTRY

Bunny Williams
Falls Village, Connecticut

With an appreciation of beauty developed growing up in the countryside around Charlottesville, Virginia, interior designer, gardener, and author Bunny Williams was destined to make the world more beautiful—inside and out. "My mother, aunts, and everyone I knew just loved their houses. My mother was a passionate gardener. She grew all kinds of vegetables and had a cutting garden for flowers and an old apple orchard with two acres of daffodils underneath that I would play among and gather up in big handfuls for bouquets."

Just out of school, Bunny went to work at the New York City antiques shop Stair & Company, which she credits with training her eye to recognize styles and periods of antique furniture and decorative arts. Next, she spent twenty-two years at the firm of two of the masters of the universe of decorating, Sister Parish and Albert Hadley, which she fondly refers to as "The University of Parish-Hadley." Thus prepared, she struck out on her own in 1988 and opened Bunny Williams Interior Design.

With a successful design firm, her own line of furnishings and accessories, and several coffee-table books, Williams is a blur of constant motion. But on weekends, whenever possible, she slows down and retreats with her husband, antiques dealer and aficionado John Rosselli, to their storybook country home in Falls Village, Connecticut.

In Bunny's interiors, flowers almost always play a role—trailing across a bank of windows on a winsome chintz, in a soft print on a sumptuous upholstered arm chair, as the subject of a painting, or even just a bouquet on a pillow. "For

me, flowers and plants make a room come alive. I use floral fabrics although I try to avoid the 'garden on a chair' look. I prefer old document patterns that are softly faded or have a slightly odd coloring—colors we don't typically think of for flowers, such as blues and browns for instance, to keep floral fabrics from becoming too predictable."

Bunny's approach to fresh flowers leans toward a more straightforward, uncontrived look. She is fond of using repetition, such as a collection of her homegrown ferns or succulents on the dining table, and favors the simplicity of monochromatic designs either with a single variety or different varieties, still all in the same color.

And when spending time at her home in the Connecticut countryside, she has but to stroll in her gardens, where she can cut from among the lilacs, viburnums, hydrangeas, and roses blooming in summer. Then, in early fall, dahlias and zinnias linger, and Bunny looks to them for more autumnal shades of oranges, rusts, and reds, and often arranges them in her copper lusterware.

From a grand-scale antique faux marble urn to a diminutive creamware pitcher, Bunny has an extensive collection of containers, organized by color, that makes arranging almost anything a snap. "I've also been known to just gather up branches and leaves," she confesses. There's a vase for that.

ABOVE: The iconic front elevation of Bunny Williams and John Rosselli's country house in Falls Village, Connecticut. OPPOSITE: Tulips from the parterre garden pick up the gold of a pillow on a blue flower-print upholstered chair in the living room. PREVIOUS PAGE: Lilacs, tulips, and Solomon's seal fill a Chinese export porcelain temple jar in the entry hall.

LEFT: A purple linen tablecloth was Bunny's point of departure for this dinner table decor. She pulled out monogrammed napkins after gathering two colors of lilacs. ABOVE: Purple pansy blooms were a last-minute addition, a lovely, simple finishing touch. FOLLOWING SPREAD, LEFT PAGE, CLOCKWISE FROM TOP LEFT: Bunny cuts from the late spring garden to arrange in a grand-scale faux marble urn—one of her staples in the "barn." The designer artfully arranges lilacs, tulips, and Solomon's seal in trellised cachepots as centerpieces. A graphic blue-and-white floral wall covering in a guest bath. RIGHT PAGE: Bunny fills her bedroom with flowers—on her bed, an antique floral suzani throw; on her bedside table, a bouquet of porcelain violets (by her friend Clare Potter); and on the wall, an antique floral still life.

BUNNY'S PICKS FOR LIVING FLORAL
ARRANGING

I keep a couple of cachepots on hand for potted plants. They're great for when I want to bring in a flowering plant from the terrace, or pick up a potted plant at Home Depot for an instant lovely arrangement.

Proper scale is so important. If someone gives me a beautiful large arrangement, I'll often cut it down to size and put it in one of my own containers. If I'm going to have a big arrangement, it's in the entry or in a larger-scale space, not on the dining room table. Guests must be able to see each other to talk.

I like to place pretty, little sweet-smelling posies in the powder room, and a larger arrangement in the entrance hall to welcome guests. I have a few key places in the living room. I like to be able to see, smell, and appreciate flowers, but I don't want to have so many that it looks like a photo shoot.

I've never met a flower I didn't like. It's all about appropriate-ness and how the flowers are used. I'm not wild about birds-of-paradise in my New York City apartment, but when I see them in a tropical garden, I think they're fabulous.

ABOVE: This corner of Bunny's living room speaks volumes about her nuanced use of color, shape, scale, and restraint: the lone green-and-white stem of Solomon's seal in a rustic bud vase with an understated picture by Paul Maze, an aubergine-colored glass hurricane lantern and antique bone box, both from John Rosselli, and the chair from Bunny Williams Home covered in a Quadrille fabric with over embroidery all render a quietly interesting effect. OPPOSITE: A coveted spot, Bunny's apricot-toned upstairs guest room in the barn is marked with a floral imprint: the antique flower-laden textiles on the bed skirt and canopy were purchased from Brigitte Singh on a trip to India. The floral-patterned fabric on the upholstered chair is by Robert Kime. And fresh geraniums on one chest and a posy of white roses in a julep cup by the bed weave in fragrant fresh flowers.

FLORAL ARRANGEMENT
HOW-TOS

MIMI BROWN

New York, New York

A talented Southerner in New York City, Mimi Brown started her life
in flowers and parties helping out a floral designer on the weekends while
in law school in Alabama. (She now heads Mimi Brown Studio in
New York City.) It was soon apparent to all, including Mimi, that she
was destined to leave the law and devote herself to developing her artistic
side. While running a floral design studio in Birmingham, she moonlighted
as mechanics editor in the early years of *Flower* magazine. Reprising
that role, Mimi walks us through the steps to create four of her favorite
easy-to-assemble floral arrangements to dress up your home.

SPRING BOUQUET

It's the season when flowers shine their brightest, as if shouting that they're back after a cold winter. A big bouquet of spring blooms will elicit joy in any space, indoors or out. This one in a *faux bois* pitcher, with blousy and wispy blooms in blush and white, is a vision of springtime.

snips • pitcher • Queen Anne's lace • hydrangeas • Japanese ranunculuses
'Butterfly' ranunculuses • tulips • sweet peas • ranunculuses

STEP 1: Start the arrangement with the Queen Anne's lace. Strip the foliage off the stems, and then cut off the parts of the flowers that are only green. The design will look better with mostly white Queen Anne's lace—otherwise the flowers will start to look like a weed.

STEP 2: Snip the ends of the stems, making them varying heights. Then place them in the pitcher so that they fan out. We're using the Queen Anne's lace as greenery, which is why it's the first material included.

STEP 3: Next, move on to the hydrangeas. As you did with the Queen Anne's lace, cut these at varying heights, but they should all be a little shorter. Because hydrangeas need so much water, split the ends of the stems with your snips so they can drink the water more easily. It's the best way to hydrate them.

STEP 4: The types of ranunculus I selected are pretty big, with their flowers having the largest face in this design, so I include them next. These should be cut so that some are taller than others. Turn the pitcher as you go, and place them throughout. It looks good when one or two are sticking up slightly higher than the rest.

STEP 5: Snip the ends of the tulip stems, and strip off the lower leaves. Wild, loose tulips give nice lines, so place them all around, with some spraying out from the lower half of the design. One trick is to manually open the tulips by flipping open the outer petals, as if unwrapping them. Do this gently to avoid damaging the petals.

STEP 6: Sweet peas are delicate and can be easily damaged if added early on, so save these for the end. If there are any brown blooms, simply snip them off. Finish with the smaller variety of ranunculus. The small buds add whimsy, so be sure to include those, as well.

STEP 7: It's fine to play with the arrangement at the end. If any of the flowers feel crowded, snip them again, spreading them out a bit. Make sure the holes are filled, including around the lip of the pitcher. I also like to crouch down to see what the arrangement looks like at eye level. It's not going to look perfect—and that's what we want.

GROUPING OF THREE

The ever-romantic French hand-tied bouquet is a florist staple. There's a simple art to it that makes this classic design easier to create than it looks. Here, I've made a happy trio to march down the table. In cement pots from a local garden shop, they look fresh as ever.

snips • three ceramic pots • floral tape • hellebores • roses • spray roses
tulips • large face ranunculuses • 'Green Trick' chrysanthemums • mini daffodils • muscaris

STEP 1: The secret to making a hand-tied bouquet is all in the crossing of the stems. Start with the hellebores, but first remove the lower leaves. (This goes for all of the materials. Strip the foliage ahead of time.) Hold one stem in front of you, and place another one in front of it so that, together, they are in the shape of an X.

STEP 2: Turn the bundle slightly, with both crossed stems in one hand. With the other hand, add another stem in front so that the bundle makes an X-like shape. Turn it again, putting the newest crossed stem in your hand with the bundle. Continue adding hellebore stems one at a time, and then move on to the roses.

STEP 3: Continue with the roses and spray roses, and then add the tulips. Constantly rotate the bouquet, adding the stems around the outer edges. Hold the bundle out in front of you so that you can better see which side you want to add to next. It's also fine to thread a tulip down in through the top.

STEP 4: After the big elements have been added, including the ranunculuses and fluffy green chrysanthemums, the stems should be fanning out nicely. Now it's time to secure everything together. I usually use wire, but you can also use floral tape as I've done here. Make sure it's tightly wrapped around a few times.

STEP 5: A traditional French hand-tied bouquet should be able to stand on its own, so the stems should be cut perfectly flat. Because I'm putting the bouquets in containers, the cut doesn't have to be exact. Don't be afraid to cut the stems more than once to get the length right for the height of the container. After completing all three bouquets, place them in the water-filled containers.

STEP 6: I purposely left out the mini daffodils and the muscaris until the very end, because they're too delicate and small to be tightly bundled with the other flowers. Before working with the mini daffodils, pull off the papery brown part of each stem—just give it a gentle tug downwards.

STEP 7: Though each hand-tied bouquet is technically already finished, it's fine to add in additional elements (such as the mini daffodils and muscaris here) after they've been placed in the containers. Thread them through and down so that the end of each stem touches the water. Also make sure the end result looks nice and full, and fill in around the rim where needed.

211

TABLE RUNNER

Low and lush is the name of the game for party flowers that wow guests and still allow for eye contact and good conversation. Any color combination will do, but pink is pretty and makes an impact.

snips · a few blocks of floral foam · hydrangeas · dusty miller · lamb's ears · hellebore foliage · peonies
roses · garden roses · ranunculuses · scabiosas · sweet peas · parrot tulips

STEP 1: Because these flowers are going in floral foam, they need to drink well beforehand. Hydrangeas especially need lots of water, so it's ideal to let them drink for twenty-four hours prior to making the runner. Snip each woody stem down the middle in about a two-inch slit to allow it to soak up the water more easily.

STEP 2: The number of caged blocks of floral foam is determined by the length of your table. (We used four for this runner.) Soak them well in water before starting. They can be wired together, but we opted for a looser look. Always start with greenery, such as the dusty miller, lamb's ears, and hellebore foliage. Snip the stems first, and then place them throughout the design.

STEP 3: After evenly adding the greenery (including on the sides of each block), add the hydrangeas, because they are the flowers with the biggest faces. First cut each stem at an angle. Typically you might have fewer hydrangea stems, so place them strategically. (We included five for this runner.)

STEP 4: Next add the peonies, and when you snip the stems, don't forget that you can cut off the lower leaves to be used as additional greenery. Then it's time to add the rose varieties, including the big garden roses. The thorns can be sharp, so just pop them off after snipping each stem to the desired length. Add the roses on all sides.

STEP 5: Ranunculus stems can be quite delicate, so gently place them in the foam. You can even dig little holes for each stem. Don't forget to include the small ranunculus buds.

STEP 6: The scabiosas and sweet peas both have thin stems, so place them carefully. Both of these flowers should be left taller in a few places. The sweet peas especially should be dancing up a little bit.

STEP 7: The parrot tulips are the last flowers to be added. They should be swirling around the outside of the runner. Finally, after you've added all of your materials and the runner is in place, fill in with greenery around the edges so that no floral foam is showing.

NO–FUSS NOSEGAY

Beauty often lies in simplicity, and this small but mighty nosegay proves that one or two types of flowers are all that's needed to create an impressive design. Clematis, from buds to fully open blossoms, and just-picked pansies marry for a look that feels effortless, gardeny, and fresh.

snips • a clear glass vase • garden pansies • clematis buds

STEP 1: Start with the pansies, as they'll make up the bulk of the arrangement and play the lead role. (These were handpicked from the garden, but they're also available from most local garden shops or flower wholesalers.) First, cut each stem at an angle, which will allow it to drink more easily in the vase.

STEP 2: The stems should be long enough to reach the water but short enough for the small vessel. No leaves should be underwater, because they'll cause bacteria that makes flowers die faster—simply pull off any leaves that are too low on the stem. Neither a wire nor a tape grid are necessary because the thick pansy stems can make a natural structure to hold the other flowers. Just cross them in the water.

STEP 3: Clematis are certainly beautiful—buds that are not fully open take on a completely different look. Remove any damaged leaves, and leave the good-looking ones alone. Then snip off the bottom of each stem, and place the flowers throughout the design so that they playfully peek out from the pansies.

214

TULIP CACHEPOT

This beloved Dutch bulb was so coveted in the early seventeenth century that it was said to be more valuable than even some of the finest houses in Amsterdam. Today, the spring staple takes on a much more casual vibe, as seen here in this French cachepot. It's refreshing to see tulips loosely arranged in such an attainable way.

snips · tole jardinière · chicken wire · floral tape · a few varieties of tulips in oranges, peaches, and pinks

STEP 1: Cut a section of chicken wire big enough to fit inside the cachepot after it's scrunched up a bit. Fold it in and push it down inside. The wire will support each tulip stem in the arrangement.

STEP 2: Once the chicken wire is placed inside, remove the metal liner that comes with the cachepot. Then secure the wire to the liner by taping two strips of floral tape over it in a cross shape. The liner needs to be completely dry in order for the tape to stick, so don't pour any water into the liner until this step is completed.

STEP 3: Now it's time to add the tulips, but first each one should be stripped of its outermost leaves. After picking up each tulip, gently peel down and pull off the leaves—this is strictly an aesthetic decision, so leave as many leaves on the stems as you like. (As I like to see some of the shape of each stem, I remove most of the leaves.) Do this as you work—not all at once. Be sure, though, to leave some of the leaves on the tulip stems because we are not adding other greenery. Then snip the end of each tulip at an angle.

STEP 4: I've chosen a mix of oranges, peaches, and pinks, and I prefer to place all of one variety before moving on to the next. Note that all of the tulips should be pretty much the same height except for a few that can be cut shorter or kept taller for variety. After placing the orange and peachy varieties, it's time for the deep pinks, which are double tulips. Everything should be pretty much the same height except for a few, which should be shorter and taller.

STEP 5: After adding the deep pink tulips, finish with the lighter pink variety. This variety has some white on the petals, which gives it a little extra interest. It's fine to manually open a tulip if it looks too tightly closed. Very gently flip back the outer petals. If a petal starts to split, don't worry—it happens.

STEP 6: Sometimes the tulips will fall as you go, and that's fine. Let some droop, but remove them if they look tired and then keep arranging as you see fit. In the end, the tulips should look as though they're naturally growing out of the container. And remember to place a few around the perimeter. It's important to make sure no chicken wire is visible.

HOW-TO
MATERIALS

Tools
1. snips 2. foam blocks 3. floral frogs
4. chicken wire 5. floral tape

Spring Bouquet
1. Queen Anne's lace 2. 'Butterfly' ranunculuses 3. sweet peas
4. hydrangeas 5. tulips 6. ranunculuses

Grouping of Three
1. mini daffodils 2. hellebores 3. spray roses 4. muscaris 5. tulips
6. roses 7. 'Green Trick' chrysanthemums 8. ranunculuses

Table Runner

1. dusty miller 2. peonies 3. scabiosas 4. roses
5. lamb's ears 6. hydrangeas 7. ranunculuses 8. sweet peas
9. parrot tulips 10. hellebore foliage

No-Fuss Nosegay

1. garden pansies 2. clematis buds

Tulip Cachepot

1. Residence tulip 2. Crossfire tulip 3. Jan Buis tulip
4. Apricot parrot tulip 5. Cerise parrot tulip

RESOURCES

NAMES OF DESIGNERS FOLLOWS BOOK ORDER

ELAINE GRIFFIN
elainegriffin.com
Saint Simons 912-434-1244
NYC 212-666-2033

CORNELIA GUEST
corneliaguest.com
212-717-1979

RICHARD KEITH LANGHAM
richardkeithlangham.com
212-759-1212

RENNY REYNOLDS AND JACK STAUB
hortulusfarm.com
215-598-0550

ELIZABETH LOCKE
elizabethlocke.com
540-837-2215

CHESIE BREEN
cell 917-538-7750 (preferred)
212-535-5518

CHARLOTTE MOSS
charlottemoss.com
212-308-7088

ASHLEY WHITTAKER
ashleywhittakerdesign.com
212-650-0024

PARDIS AND FRANK STITT
highlandsbarandgrill.com
205-939-1400

SCHUYLER SAMPERTON
samperton.com
323-655-6603

JAMES CARTER
jamesfcarter.com
205-871-7873

WENDY WURTZBURGER
roarandrabbit.com
215-454-5500

ALEX HITZ
alexhitz.com
917-854-6724

MINDY RICE
mindyrice.com
310-308-3735

BRYAN BATT
bryanbatt.com
504-891-2424

REBECCA VIZARD
rebeccavizard.com
318-766-4950

SYBIL SYLVESTER
wildflowerdesigns.net
office 205-322-1311
cell 205-229-2416

REBECCA GARDNER
rebecca-gardner.com
912-335-2687

BARRY DIXON
barrydixon.com
540-341-8501

P. ALLEN SMITH
pallensmith.com
501-376-1894

SUZANNE RHEINSTEIN
suzannerheinstein.com
310-550-8900

CALDER CLARK
calderclark.com
843-641-0055

THOMAS JAYNE
jaynedesignstudio.com
212-838-9080

FRANCES SCHULTZ
francesschultz.com

CHRISTOPHER SPITZMILLER
christopherspitzmiller.com
212-563-3030

ALEX PAPACHRISTIDIS
alexpapachristidis.com
212-588-1777

TARA GUÉRARD
taraguerardsoiree.com
843-577-5006

BUNNY WILLIAMS
bunnywilliams.com
212-207-4040

MIMI BROWN
mimibrownstudio.com
917-428-7813

A FEW OF MY FAVORITE THINGS AND WHERE TO FIND THEM

MARGOT SHAW
Pages 14–15: Paintings by (top) James Locke,
(on mantel, left to right) Jill Hooper, Ashley
Spotswood, and R. Orr

CORNELIA GUEST
Page 27: Throw on chair by Turkish T
Black-and-white pitcher *Country Estate*
by Juliska
Cloth on table by Les Indiennes

ELIZABETH LOCKE
Page 48: *Classic Square Planters* in
Lead Grey by Pennoyer Newman;
pennoyernewman.com

CHARLOTTE MOSS
Page 59: Plates *Nancy* by Charlotte Moss
for Pickard

ASHLEY WHITTAKER
Page 69: Botanical patterned fabric
on table *Grace* from Jasper by
Michael S. Smith
Faux bois plates by Ross Sveback

SYBIL SYLVESTER
Pages 130–31: Containers on mantel by
Vitriluxe at A'mano in Birmingham, Alabama
Page 132: All wallpapers by Ashley
Woodson Bailey

MIMI BROWN
Pages 210–11: Cement pots from Shoppe
shoppebham.com

RIGHT: A detail of Charlotte Moss's summer luncheon table, including vintage floral-painted water glasses, wicker covered salt and pepper shakers, and a gathering of her luscious garden roses.

ACKNOWLEDGMENTS

I must first acknowledge that the terribly hackneyed phrase "It takes a village" could have been coined, not only for this book, *Living Floral*, but for *Flower*, the magazine that inspired it. Neither would have seen the light of day had it not been for a laundry list of committed family, friends, and publishing professionals, all of whom I thank below.

FAMILY

My parents, Caroline and Conrad, long departed, who exposed me to beauty and culture from early on.

My husband, Gates, who once asked me, "What are you going to do with all your talents?" and who remains my greatest encourager, sounding board, traveling companion, and secret weapon.

My brother, Conrad, a fellow creative who has been there, advised and championed me since childhood, and completely gets what I'm doing.

His wife, Peggy, who is always up for a *Flower* trip, event, or project, and opens up her house for a photo shoot at the drop of a hat—witness the "how-to" section in this book.

My daughters Hansell, Elizabeth, and Westcott, who are all amazing, encouraging, and patient.

My uncle Allen, who, as a fellow writer and creative, has been a key player and cheerleader.

My cousin Evie Vare, Garden Club of America mainstay, who has been a rich source of wise counsel and floral expertise.

And my other cousins Lisa, Rena, Studie, Nina, Kate, and Walker, who are true-blue and have given lifelong love and support.

FLOWER FRIENDS

Karen Carroll, who, while editor in chief of the now sorely missed *Southern Accents*, listened to my crazy idea to start a flower magazine, gave me invaluable guidance, and then later joined our team—and whose writing appears in these pages.

Lydia Somerville, who was a senior editor at *Southern Accents* and didn't laugh in my face when I pronounced that she would one day be writing for me—her words also grace these pages.

Michael Mundy, whom I met while I was "flowering" a *Southern Accents* shoot and agreed to photograph for me if I ever started the magazine I was dreaming of, and who has been my first-call photographer ever since.

Louise Agee Wrinkle, the legendary Southern plants woman and gardener, who took an interest in my humble efforts and gave out of her deep pool of knowledge and experience whenever asked.

Sybil Sylvester, of Wildflower Designs, who, after working with me to "flower" my oldest daughter's home wedding, took me on as a forty-six-year-old intern and poured her knowledge and vision into a complete neophyte.

Tim Young, who, as editor of *Portico Magazine* in Birmingham, helped me with all the infrastructure I would need to launch *Flower* and stayed on for years to continue to help shepherd the project.

Julie Durkee, who, as she was leafing through the pages of an early issue of *Flower* at my neighbor's house, casually mentioned that she'd like to sell ads for me and is now not only our publisher but also the driving force behind my deciding to take on a book.

Alice Welsh Doyle, who has contributed her unerring editorial instincts to *Living Floral*.

Ellen Padgett, who hears my voice and chimes in, gets my vision and adds some of hers, and has designed the layout of this book accordingly and beautifully.

Katie Baker Lasker, advisory board member and longtime friend, who has through the years urged—no, badgered—me to write.

Abby Waller Braswell, stellar former *Flower* managing editor, who produced the How-To's.

Some integral past and present *Flower* team players: Melissa Brown, Liz Young, John Cobbs, the late Tom Morris, Liz Major, Julie Cole Miller, Katherine Perry Glenn, Kelly Baker, Pamela Hanes Hollon, Catherine Booker Jones, Elizabeth Peelen, Mallory Towns, Claire Cormany, Jena Henderson, Alexandra Schmitt, Ryan Gainey, Jennel O'Brien, Jessica Cohen, Jason Burnett, Gregory Keyes Jr., Kevin Blechman, DeLisa McDaniels, Patrick Toomey, Sara Taylor, Amanda Smith Fowler, Kirk Forrester, Kate Johnson, Silvia Rider, Greg Keyes Sr., and Michael Trucks.

Joe Smith and Jane Sloan, both now gone, who were two of my greatest allies and advocates in Nashville, Tennessee, and beyond.

Charlotte Moss, who came to dinner years ago and decided to contribute to and champion my efforts, and who is an incredible mentor.

Carleton Varney, who, from the early days of my publishing life, has been a steadfast friend and booster.

Cornelia Guest, whom I met in a hotel gym and who proceeded to encourage and participate in my publishing efforts with generosity and enthusiasm.

The Reepicheeps—you know who you are.

RIZZOLI

My editor, Sandy Gilbert Freidus, who has been an inspiration. I'm immensely grateful for her willingness to take a chance on me. Her pitch-perfect editing as well as her lighthearted and light-handed approach have been huge blessings.

Deborah Gardner, a quietly brilliant editor and genuinely lovely person.

Pam Sommers, for getting the word out.

Elizabeth Smith and Susan Homer copyeditors extraordinaire, who tussled doggedly with the nuances of "botanical-ese," not to mention my sometimes random syntax and use of punctuation.

And finally, Charles Miers, for saying, "Yes."

OPPOSITE: Bunny Williams fills her house with quiet floral moments like this corner of her bedroom featuring an antique tole flower arrangement, a chest with hand-painted flowers, and a fauteuil upholstered in pretty blue floral fabric.

PHOTOGRAPHY CREDITS

Edward Addeo: pages 139, 143, 145

Shyla Barcelona: pages 103–07

Carmel Brantley: pages 39–45

Kerri Brewer: page 170 (top right)

Monica Buck: pages 69–73

Chia Chong: pages 135–37

Alison Conklin: pages 93–99

Lucy Cuneo: pages 193–95

Kip Dawkins: pages 47–51

Courtesy of Barry Dixon: page 142 (top left)

Pieter Estersohn: pages 155–59, 167–70, 185

Christina Gerry: pages 28, 29

Tria Giovan: pages 173–77, 183, 184, 186, 190

Laurey W. Glenn: pages 5, 10–11, 14–15

David Hillegas: pages 32, 87–91

Tula Jeng: page 84 (top right)

Stefanie Keenan: page 156 (top right)

Raimund Koch: page 189

Erik Kvalsvik: pages 2, 140–41, 142 (top right and bottom), 144, 179–81, 197–205, 222

Julia Lynn: pages 19–25, 161–65

Kerri McCaffety: pages 115–19, 121–27

Elizabeth Messina: pages 109–13

Michael Mundy: pages 8–9, 27, 31–37, 59–65

Donna Newman: page 188

Nancy Nolan: pages 149–53

Deanie Nyman: page 157

Alex Papachristidis: page 188

Lisa Romerein: pages 6, 84

Brooke Slezak: pages 53–57

Becky Luigart-Stayner: pages 12, 75–79, 129–33, 207–19

Ivan Terestchenko: pages 81, 82, 85

William Waldron: page 171

PAGE 2: A flower-filled table in Christopher Spitzmiller's country house.

PAGE 5: French doors open up behind a rose-needlepoint Louis XVI–style French chair in my dining room.

PAGE 6: In this bright seating area, Schuyler Samperton uses floral-patterned fabric on chairs and pillows and finishes with an exuberant arrangement of pink roses.

PAGE 9: Charlotte Moss with Buddy and Daisy in her East Hampton garden.

ENDPAPERS: Caroline fabric by Charlotte Moss for Fabricut.

SEASONAL SECTION OPENERS: Michael Devine fabrics and wallpapers. For Summer: Garden Folly; for Fall: Venice; for Winter: Maze; for Spring: Petite Fleur.

First published in the United States of America in 2019
by Rizzoli International Publications, Inc.
300 Park Avenue South
New York, New York 10010
www.rizzoliusa.com

Text ©2019 Margot Shaw

2019 2020 2021 2022 / 10 9 8 7 6 5 4 3 2 1

Printed in China

ISBN-13: 978-0-8478-6362-4

Library of Congress Control Number: 2018961289

Project Editor: Sandra Gilbert
Project Manager: Kaija Markoe
Editorial Assistance: Deborah Gardner, Elizabeth Smith, and Susan Homer
Art Direction: Ellen Shanks Padgett